MARKETS,
MOBS &
MAYHEM

MARKETS, MOBS & MAYHEM

A MODERN LOOK AT THE MADNESS OF CROWDS

ROBERT MENSCHEL

John Wiley & Sons, Inc.

Published by John Wiley & Sons, Inc., Hoboken, New Jersey.
Published simultaneously in Canada.

For general information on our other products and services please contact our Customer Care Department within the U.S. at (800) 762-2974, outside the United States at (317) 572-3993 or fax (317) 572-4002.

Wiley also publishes its books in a variety of electronic formats. Some content that appears in print may not be available in electronic books.

Library of Congress Cataloging-in-Publication Data:

Menschel, Robert.
    Markets, mobs, and mayhem : a modern look at the madness of crowds /
Robert Menschel.
        p.   cm.
Includes index.
    ISBN 0-471-23327-7 (acid-free)
    1. Risk.   2. Risk—Sociological aspects.   3. Collective behavior.   4.
Financial crises.   I. Title.
    HB615 .M46 2002
    302.3—dc21

                                                                2002010798

Printed in the United States of America.

10 9 8 7 6 5 4 3 2

For Joyce, David, and Lauren

Contents

2 Rumors & Suggestions

3 Fear & Panic

4 Violence & Vigilantes

5 Leaders & Followers

Foreword

On: the contrary.

"To *Contrarians* and Libertarians everywhere," wrote the Vermont ruminator H.B. Neill in the dedication to his 1954 *Art of Contrary Thinking,* "May their numbers grow!"

That is the earliest use of the word *contrarian* that Oxford English Dictionary lexicographers have been able to find. The relatively new locution is rooted in the Latin *contra*, "opposite," and nicely defines the little band of prickly iconoclasts who swim against the tide, cut against the grain, and—in the view of the lemminglike crowd of conventional thinkers—make general nuisances of themselves, especially when they turn out to be right or get rich or find happiness.

No, our numbers have not grown in the past half century, nor in the centuries since the Dutch began to tiptoe and then to stampede through their tulip craze. That is as it should be: Different drummers cannot by definition beat their tom-toms in unison, and a "herd of individualists" is a contradiction in terms. Contrarians are a permanent minority, comfortable only in articulate opposition to the placidly received wisdom or panicked self-delusion of the majority.

Orneriness is not godliness. We are aware that the soul who sails through life serene in his solitude may be out of step not just with humanity but with reality. A desire to stand out at any cost—or,

worse, a desperation to define oneself by what one is not—such unre-
lenting negativism is fake contrarianism. Although the true contrarian resists too-popular trends with sometimes grim resolve, he or she
realizes that being plain stubborn is not necessarily being smart.

I was introduced to *Popular Delusions and the Madness of
Crowds,* the 1841 work by Charles Mackay, in a post–World War II
pre-fab dormitory at Syracuse University by my roommate, Robert
Menschel. We had come up together from the Bronx High School of
Science, where we first donned the uniform of individuality. Bob was
hooked on that strange book exposing the moods of mobs, far more
so than his assigned texts in finance courses. He would quote from his
beat-up copy of *Madness* as if it were Scripture, interrupting late-
night readings of my own freshman prose. Bob was also taken by
Ralph Waldo Emerson's aphorisms, such as "The greatest man is he
who in the midst of the crowd keeps with perfect sweetness the independence of solitude," which called for his roommate to reply, "So
leave me alone."

It's a good thing he did not. Over the generations, Bob refined
and learned to live by a philosophy of not getting carried away by
everyone else's excessive enthusiasms and not being turned off by others' fears. Applied to investments, that approach—and its resultant
over 20 percent average annual return over four decades—struck awe
in his partners at Goldman Sachs, where he became an investment
legend and built an institutional department that became the model
for Wall Street's leading investment banking houses. Then, as most
of his age cohort went all out for personal pocket lining, Menschel at
50 turned toward activist philanthropy, taking over investments for a
private foundation and significantly outperforming the Standard &
Poor averages over the past two decades. The present senior director
of Goldman Sachs put his financial and marketing acumen to work
to guide, support, and invigorate hospitals, schools, libraries, and
museums, including New York's Museum of Modern Art, where he
is now president. He is the trustiest of trustees because he stimulates
the dozen boards and investment committees he serves on and brings
his own standard of excellence to the doing of good.

Through it all, the student in him remained fascinated about the inexplicable transformations that take place in people swept up into the emotional maelstrom of a crowd. His interest was not just in economic booms and busts, marketing fads and bioterrorist fears. The theme encapsulated in the old phrase "madness of crowds" slices through politics, the media, wartime fury, and peacetime smugness. What is it about a political bandwagon that drags us along against our better judgement? Why do sober individuals become drunk with rage in a lynch mob? What makes company love misery? How does our self become transformed into mindless selfishness during a rush of events?

In this book you will find examples of dramatic reporting of egregious misjudgments, as well as advice to avoid such blunders by the wisest minds the anthologist could find. In a sense, *Markets, Mobs, and Mayhem* is what used to be called a "commonplace book," a life-long collection of answers to questions troubling an inquiring mind. In another sense, the message can be the opposite of commonplace: Herein can be found Thurberian hilarity at the sheer silliness of unreasoning fear, as well as wonderment about the promotion of human hatred that still shames every generation.

On occasion, each of us, in whatever our field, can hear the whisper of rumor and the murmur of peer pressure that, unresisted, is amplified into a roar of the crowd. Iconoclastic opinion mongers try to stay alert to the undertow of conventional wisdom; we close our ears to the media drumbeat that drowns out all other sound until we find ourselves splashing about in what keepers of shark tanks in aquariums call a "feeding frenzy." That sets up the Contrarian Moment, when someone apart from the crowd coolly reports the Emperor to be clothes free; the pendulum of public opinion swings back; the Cheshire cat disappears leaving nothing but its chagrin; and the pack races off in another direction.

To be sure, the crowd is not always crazy. Patriotic fervor can be directed to good ends. A people's collective wisdom deserves at least some respect. Rudyard Kipling's classic salute to individuality, "If," is quoted at the end of this book to hail the inner-directed person who stands fast against the world's panic. But it has been savagely parodied: "If you can keep your head when all others about you are losing theirs—then perhaps you don't understand the seriousness of the situation."

That said, by far the greatest danger to good sense, good citizenship, and the good life is a slavish subjection to tides and trends. The episodes, commentaries, and apothegms that follow, enriched with the observations of an author who has lived up to his beliefs, make us think twice about getting along by going along.

When you're sure there's no way to go but up, look down. When everybody's blazing away, hold your fire. When everyone agrees the future is hopeless, invest. When you feel the thrill of a demagogue's message, don't join the party. And when you feel yourself being carried away on the shoulders of a cheering crowd, carry yourself right back before it's too late.

—William Safire

Preface:
An Epidemic of Fear

Last year, an anthrax "epidemic" swept the nation. Not an epidemic of actual cases: Those were mercifully few and geographically confined. But an epidemic of fear brought on by the few cases and the multiplier effects of natural trepidation, a media machine operating in overdrive, and a world newly connected by the Internet.

"Anthrax Scare Closes High Court: Treatment Urged for Thousands." So read the lead headline in the *Washington Post*. News junkies who had the stamina to track the article 11 paragraphs and 14 pages into the newspaper learned that the anthrax spores in question had been found in an air filter at a Supreme Court warehouse at an undisclosed location in suburban Prince George's County, not at the main Supreme Court building next to the U.S. Capitol in downtown Washington, D.C. But news junkies are rare, and news inflation these days is everywhere.

For the relatively few people who then worked at the Supreme Court warehouse, the anthrax story represented a clear and present danger. For the thousands of Washingtonians urged to take treatment, the article was bound to hit home, too. There's nothing like being handed a bottle of green Cipro capsules to concentrate the attention. Employees at the main Supreme Court building, including the nine justices, had cause for alarm also: Material flows back and forth between the warehouse and the main site, and sure enough, four days later, a few anthrax spores were detected where the Court traditionally meets although the justices had by then moved on to a new venue, just to be safe.

But for millions of other Americans who read about the Supreme Court and anthrax in their own newspaper or, more likely, saw and heard about it on television, the story seemed to have almost as direct an effect. If those big shots, why not me? If the nation's capital, why not Nashville or Tulsa, Fresno or Fargo? In New York City, so many people were checking themselves into emergency rooms to see if their flulike symptoms were the onset of fatal anthrax poisoning that a hospital system already shaken by the attacks on the World Trade Center seemed ready to collapse, a victim this time of public hysteria. And still the story wouldn't die. Led by a phalanx of instant experts and alarmed talking heads on CNN and CNBC, Fox News and MSNBC, and a host of Internet sites, the anthrax panic continued to spread until it seemed barely safe for people to leave home, much less draw a breath of air or even check their e-mail.

So goes the madness of crowds.

A second epidemic of fear was also at work, in some ways an even more threatening one: a fear that the good economic times were over, that the stock market had turned downward not just for a breather but for years, maybe even a decade or more to come.

For 10-plus years, investors had stampeded up the hill, lured on by absurd spikes in the share value of companies that had virtually no underlying support, driven into a frenzy by media reports that seemed to promise an endless upward spiral, and teased on by normally soberminded business analysts who seemed to have forgotten or never learned the first thing about history. (A personal favorite: the book *Dow 36,000* by James K. Glassman and Kevin A. Hassett, which predicted a 300 percent increase in the Dow Jones Industrial Average at the same time the DJIA was collapsing by nearly 30 percent.) Investors soon stampeded down the same hill, even faster than they had climbed it, and as always, the truth was somewhere in between the extremes.

We go to bed one night, and the federal government is sporting a surplus in excess of $4 trillion. We wake up the next morning, it seems, and the $4-trillion-plus surplus has disappeared. Meanwhile, federal budget officials are working overtime to project their figures out 5 and 10 years when they can't even tell what the bottom line will be over the next 15 days.

Conventional wisdom says that the long-term problems of the Social Security system can be fixed by allowing Americans to invest their government-held retirement funds in the stock market. Then along comes the spectacular bankruptcy of Enron, the Houston-based energy trader, and conventional wisdom suddenly declares the idea dangerous, even heretical.

When the Japanese economy was booming along, everyone knew the reason why: Government, banks, industry, even workers were all working from the same script. When the Japanese economy went bust, everyone knew the reason why, too: There was too much lock-step thinking, too few independent voices. It's enough to make the sudden twists and turns of a herd of stampeding cattle seem reasonable.

In the summer of 2000, I spent a weekend in elegant East Hampton, on the eastern end of Long Island. The event included a luncheon hosted by a former partner of mine at the investment firm of Goldman Sachs, where I have worked nearly my entire professional life. Among the eight of us in attendance was Lawrence Summers, who had replaced Robert Rubin as Bill Clinton's secretary of the treasury and would soon become president of Harvard. The group had come together on an almost annual basis to bounce around questions about the stock market and the economy, and Larry had remembered my aversion to purchasing high-multiples technology stocks from previous meetings.

"How about Cisco?" he asked me this time. "Do you still believe that the tech sector is a bad investment?"

It was an entirely reasonable question. A darling of high-tech investors, Cisco was then selling at a fat $66 a share. But I had no intention of shifting ground.

"Yes," I said. "It's selling at 200 times earnings. Who can believe in that?"

This was a group of shrewd investors, people who had made huge amounts of money for themselves and their clients in the stock market, and to a person they disagreed with me. Cisco is something you give to your grandchildren, they countered. It couldn't go anywhere but up. A little more than a year later, Cisco was down more than 80 percent from its high, which means that it would have to go up 500 percent to get back to where it sat when it was a "can't-miss, pass-on-to-the-grandkids" buy.

So, too, goes the madness of crowds, even when the smart money has every reason to know better.

Finally, there is a third epidemic of fear hovering over America, an amorphous one but perhaps the most debilitating of all: the fear of terrorism, an overwhelming concern that the Islamic extremists who struck at the World Trade Center and the Pentagon on September 11, 2001—and who might well have struck the White House or the Capitol save for the bravery of the passengers on United Airlines Flight 93—are only the tip of the iceberg.

From everything I read and hear, the extremists are indeed just a tip. The armies of hate seem to have a boundless supply of young people, all of them ready to sacrifice their lives on the front lines. But from everything I know, too, we in the United States and in the Western world have both the knowledge and the will to successfully combat such terrorists and to do so without compromising our societies and the beliefs they are built on. The madness of crowds, though, cares little about the coolness of the reason.

Logically, it's easy to counter all those epidemics of fear. A month into the anthrax terror, there were four documented deaths from spore inhalation, and another 14 cases diagnosed, half of those of the less dangerous cutaneous variety of infection. Were the deaths to rise 800 fold in the months ahead, the total would still be less than the 3,300 Americans who died of polio in 1952, of nearly 58,000 reported cases of the disease, and less than half the 7,000 people who died in 1916, the worst year for polio in American history. In fact, the odds of contracting anthrax poisoning appear to be far less than the odds of being hit by lightning, even if you are carrying a golf club in your hand.

I don't mean to discount the suffering visited upon those who contracted anthrax poisoning or upon their families and loved ones, either, or the complexity of battling a substance about which so little seems to be known. But numbers do tell a story, and what they tell us is that anthrax is far from epidemic proportions by any measurement other than by the fear induced.

Over 13,000 Americans died along the lower Mississippi River in 1858 from an outbreak of yellow fever. Between 1981 and June 2000, the United States recorded nearly 440,000 deaths from AIDS. The flu epidemic of 1918 and 1919 killed about 550,000 Americans—about one in every 21 people then alive in the country. Those are epidemics. Anthrax was a panic.

Numbers tell, or should tell, a similarly reassuring story about the stock market crash that followed the Internet-driven bubble. Yes, by mid-2002, the Dow average was down nearly a quarter from its high of April 2000. Yes, Standard & Poor's average of 500 stocks was down 28 percent for the first 10 months of 2001 alone. Yes, the Nasdaq average, having climbed higher during the market bubble than the other averages, fell faster and more steeply once investors decided they could no longer support such lunacy. But as we'll shortly see, if there is one uncomplicated and consistent lesson that equity markets teach, it is this: They are self-correcting in the extreme. Rather than panic as the stock market plunged, investors should have looked upon it as an opportunity to buy true value.

As for the threat of terrorism and of an Islamic jihad against the industrialized West, we've faced more formidable enemies and been far less well prepared for the task. Writing in the October 28, 2001, *New York Times,* the Pulitzer Prize–winning historian David Kennedy reminded readers that, by early 1942, there seemed little hope anywhere for Americans. Across the Atlantic, most of Western Europe had fallen to the Nazis. The Soviet Union seemed sure to go next with Great Britain not far behind. Across the Pacific, the British were about to surrender their huge garrison at Singapore to the Japanese.

America's Atlantic coast was so besieged by German U-boats that shipping was threatening to grind to a halt. On the other side of the continent, the massive damage at Pearl Harbor had left California so seemingly vulnerable to a Japanese advance guard that the Rose Bowl game had been moved 2,500 miles east to the football stadium at Duke University.

"In the face of these threats," Kennedy writes, "a deeply isolationist and unprepared United States could muster only the resources of an economy badly blighted by the decade-long Depression, a skeletal Navy gutted at Pearl Harbor and a poorly equipped, untrained Army of barely a million men. . . . A bleaker, more hopeless, picture is difficult to imagine. Yet we know how that story ended. Less than four years after Pearl Harbor the United States had utterly vanquished its foes."

So this story shall end as well, and along the way we will wring out the excesses that have shaken society in so many ways: excesses of valuation in the stock market, excesses of hype in the media that have fed the human predilection toward overreacting to every new twist in the passing scene, excesses of confidence that the problems of other nations wouldn't become the problems of our own, excesses of grandeur in the corporate world that led to staggering CEO salaries and self-aggrandizing office towers.

At some level, nearly all of us knew that it was wrong to be paying a mere $6 an hour to the security guards who screen airplane passengers and their carry-on luggage. The Federal Aviation Administration knew the screening was inadequate. The pilots who flew the planes were so convinced of the inadequacy that they took to standing outside the cockpit whenever they could, to eyeball the passengers as they boarded. Yet it took the deaths of 3,000 Americans to show us just how wrong it was and how sloppy we had allowed our security systems to become.

In time, too, we'll even put that number—3,000 dead in one morning of attacks—in perspective. Perhaps as many as 2,000 Americans died on April 27, 1865, when the steamship *Sultana* exploded on the Mississippi River. Most of the dead, in a nation less than an eighth the size that it is today, were emaciated Union prisoners, finally on their way home after four years of Civil War. All in all, the *Sultana* was an epic disaster: Expressed as a percentage of the total U.S. population, those 2,000 or so deaths would be closer to 16,000 today. Yet the explosion received relatively scant attention in its own day and is all but forgotten to modern history. Americans had seen too much death by April 1865; they were looking forward to living again. We modern Americans will look forward to living again, too, and what now seems overwhelming will find its place and fade with memory.

Here's one more prediction you can take to the bank. Once we've wrung out the excesses, once we've found a way to deal with the staggering numbers and tidied up around the edges of our messy society, some new madness or set of madnesses is sure to come sweeping across the landscape and grab us all again because nothing is more in the nature of crowds than that: A crowd wants to be led, and often it doesn't much care where. The best we as individuals can hope to do is to learn to stand apart and to keep our own sense of order when disorder is all around us.

Most of us got our first lessons in crowd behavior early in life. Maybe we took a dare and swiped a piece of candy from the corner store. Or we smoked a first cigarette because everyone else was puffing away and we wanted to be part of the group. Or we joined our peers in taunting a weaker classmate on the playground. The instinct is almost universal, and the first line of defense when we're caught and forced to face our parents is almost always the same, too: "All the other kids were doing it!"

I know that was my reaction when I was first dragged before the tribunal of my mother for some similar infraction. I can remember her response to this day, more than half a century later: "If your friends jumped off a bridge, would you jump off one, too?" Trick question! I wanted to shout. But back then, I probably wasn't certain if I would jump or not.

The peer pressure that so drives us when we are kids is supposed to disappear as we achieve adulthood. We've made it through college, earned our stripes, claimed a slot in the work world. We put our name on mortgages and now carry around a wallet full of credit cards.

Surely, we're our own person after all that. But instead of going away, peer pressure is more likely to broaden and deepen. The desire for group acceptance that so compelled us in our teen years becomes the drive to professional and personal success. Instead of the most popular boys and girls in the classroom determining the norms, we discover that there's now a whole slew of enforcers.

We ingratiate ourselves with maître d's we don't really like because we're afraid that, if we don't, we'll get a bad table. We fail to speak out at a staff meeting for fear we'll offend a supervisor and not get the promotion. We act on stock tips we know better than to trust because, just in case they prove right, we don't want to be left behind.

Most of the time these compromises with our inner self do no visible harm. Community requires a certain amount of going along to get along. Problems come when we sacrifice our individual will and volition to the will and volition of the group—when we pool our small compromises to empower the crowd. The larger the crowd, and the more forcefully led it is, the easier it is to abandon individual will, and the greater becomes the collective power of our separate compromises.

Standing on the street corner absorbed in our own thoughts, we might never think to look to the top of the building across the street. But if the person next to us is peering intently upward, chances are that we'll look up ourselves, and if that person has been joined by a half-dozen others, it's almost impossible not to join in. All that, of course, is benign—assuming there's not a pickpocket working the crowd—but the same principles can lead to more ominous behavior.

Individually, we might find it absurd to suspect the Arab American shopkeeper down the street of collaborating in any way with the terrorists who destroyed the World Trade Center towers and attacked the Pentagon, just as in 1941 we might have found it absurd to suspect the Japanese American nurseryman out on the highway of collaborating in any way with the terrorist air force that bombed Pearl Harbor. Or just as in 1776 we might have found it absurd to suspect the neighbor recently arrived from London of collaborating with the British redcoats. But in a crowd, individual will can weaken. The absurd becomes the possible; the possible, the probable; the probable, the certain. Swept up by the spirit of groupthink, we find ourselves boycotting the Muslim grocer, advocating internment of the Japanese American nurseryman and his wife and children, and demanding that the Tory sympathizer be drawn and quartered in the town square.

Individual common sense says that a stock selling at 200 times earnings has come unmoored from reality. Group sense says that, if 200 times, why not 400 times, by which time we'll have doubled our investment. Common sense says that over half a billion pieces of mail are delivered daily in the United States without endangering any recipients. Group sense says that one letter tainted with potential fatal spores spoils the barrel. Common sense says that the glory of America is that we are a pluralistic society, accepting of a hundred different ethnicities and a hundred different faiths. Group sense says, "America, Love It or Leave It," and starts to fire up the torches. And, yes, it has ever been so.

The present moment always feels like the only one. The past is dead; the future an enigma. *Now* is the crossroads, the threshold . . . except that the future gets continually built out of the recycled past. Stock markets today are different in degree from the stock markets of 70 years ago. Money flies around the world at the speed of light. For institutional investors, buy and sell decisions are more likely to be made by computers than by individuals. But today's stock markets are not different in kind than the ones that preceded the Great Depression or than the first stock markets of four centuries ago. Then, today, and forever more, equity markets will bring people together for the purpose of trading risk and reward.

Then, today, and forever more, investors also will go looking for someone to blame when risk and reward get so out of kilter that the roof comes caving in. The stock analysts who continued to tout Internet and telecommunications stocks even when they were wildly overvalued don't deserve any citizenship awards. Nor do the brokerage houses they worked for. Firewalls that should have stood between the advice-giving and commission-collecting sides of the businesses were missing in too many instances. But it wasn't the analysts who picked up the phones or logged on to e-trade accounts and placed the purchase orders. The system was faulty, but individuals succumbing to crowd norms made the decisions that cemented the madness in place. And that was as true of the bubble market that preceded the Great Depression as it was of the bubble market that heralded the (thankfully) lesser market collapse of our own time.

Today's news holds our eye, but history is replete with examples of actions taken by crowds that might never have been countenanced individually by most of the crowd's members. The throng that met the Beatles at Idlewild Airport on Long Island when they first landed in the United States in 1964, the shrieking crowds that greeted Elvis "the Pelvis" Presley on stage in the mid-1950s, the bobby-soxers who swooned a generation earlier over a skinny Jersey kid named Frank Sinatra—they're all examples of individuals who took their behavioral norms not from within but from the crowd they found themselves in. So, too, at a far extreme are vigilante justice, lynchings, pogroms, even genocides. And both the collective adoration of pop idols and the collective violence against those who find themselves outside the norms of the crowd have been going on since time immemorial.

The media and an interconnected world can accelerate the creation of the mass delusions that so move crowds. Orson Welles's 1938 radio dramatization of H.G. Wells's *The War of the Worlds* remains the most famous example. Despite ample disclaimers before and after the broadcast and manifest impossibilities written into the plot, large numbers of people still managed to persuade themselves that they were hearing an actual news account of a bona fide invasion from Mars. In retrospect, it's hard to miss the massive illogic of it all, but try to imagine yourself hearing a commotion outside, then being besieged by phone calls from relatives and friends, and then finally tuning in to the broadcast in progress. The air of alarm, the messages of doom, the general buzz of electricity would all conspire to lend credence to the fiction being spun on the radio.

What radio can do effectively, television can do in some ways even better. Add image to sound and throw in a brutally competitive environment struggling to reach an increasingly fragmented audience, and even the most dignified commercial news outlets can sink to a sensationalism that turns common events into causes for alarm, and causes for alarm into public panics.

Nothing can top the Internet when it comes to fostering delusion. Hundreds, even thousands of fantasies—from the Roswell, New Mexico, aliens, to complex conspiracy theories, to the fortunes to be made by purchasing stocks in companies that don't even own their own furniture—are kept alive in cyberspace by highly self-selecting audiences who commune only with each other and thus have no competing views of reality.

The media and the Internet can intensify the creation of delusions and mass crowd behavior, but they didn't invent them. A century before the personal computer, Millerites around America were selling all their worldly possessions and gathering on hilltops to await an apocalypse that never arrived. In 1962, a worker at a North Carolina textile mill reported that he had been bitten by a poisonous insect. Within a week, 62 of his fellow workers also claimed to have been bitten, and had the rash and other symptoms, including nausea, to prove it—except that, as was subsequently shown, the bug had never existed. Word of mouth had taken the suggestion and turned it into a truth strong enough to create its own reality.

Nuts? Sure, now that we know the Millerites were wrong about the end of the world and the textile workers wrong about their poisonous insect, but when it comes to crowd behavior, a little nuttiness seems only too human.

In part, whether the individual or crowd sense prevails—and whether the best or worst in human nature is brought out—depends on who's leading. Martin Luther King Jr. exhorting a quarter of a million people on the Mall in Washington to "let freedom ring, let freedom ring" was as conscious of the psyche of the crowd as Adolph Hitler had been three decades earlier when he sought to arouse the hatred of the German nation against a minority of its populace. King was appealing to the better instincts of his listeners, Hitler to the basest ones, but what both men surely knew was that where the few lead, the many often follow.

Is everyone who loots a store after some civic disturbance a thief at heart? No, but once a few leaders create a new norm of social behavior, new rules of civil conduct begin to prevail. Is everyone who rushes an enemy machine-gun nest a born hero? Again, no, but once the innately brave create the norm among their comrades, courage spreads as surely as cowardice spreads in a lynch mob. Nor is everyone who buys stocks near the top of a wildly gyrating market or sells them near the bottom a perfect, or even a motley fool. They've only bought in to a collective logic that negates what they often know individually to be the wise course.

Whether common sense or group sense prevails is a matter of what kind of crowd we're talking about. The many forms of a crowd can be charted on a scale like the progression of a fever, from inadvertent crowds, to demonstrations, rioting mobs, and worse. Rumor and suggestion act on the merging psyche of the group to drive it toward fear and panic. Unchecked, fear and panic emerge into violence or even vigilantism. The crowd is the natural haunt of the demagogue, who tries to channel its emotions toward specific targets, and in today's connected world, the demagogue can gather his audience globally.

Radio talk shows and the proliferation of TV talking heads and Internet chat rooms have created what are essentially vast decentralized crowds, media cocoons ready to take on all the characteristics and moods of physical crowds, depending on how they are swayed and how suggestible their members are. But whether the crowd exists in reality or only in virtuality, its capacity for good or ill finally comes down to the personal choices each and every one of us makes. Do we go along to get along? Do we yield our own sense to the group sense? Do we buy someone else's interpretation of events, or do we constantly test it against what we know deep down to be true?

The most dangerous part of any crowd isn't the numbers or the noise, the cause or the target. The most dangerous part is nothing more than a voice, an impulse, a notion that vibrates so strongly in the air around you that you might even think you came up with it yourself. Your mother knew it as "peer pressure"—that collision of the insecurity and suggestibility that are part of the human equipment—but whatever words we use, this power of the herd and our ability to resist it really is the final determinant. Crowds begin with individuals coming together one by one. In financial decisions as much as in audience stampedes, in matters of taste as much as in matters of ethics, in political crises as in the upswings of fads, the important thing is to shut off the pressure you may feel from outside and think for yourself.

That's what this book is for: to show you how to escape the crowd and what happens when you can't. The tension between the individual and the crowd predates all of us and will continue long after we all are gone, but the individuals who resist the pressure of their panicky peers—the ones who act on their internal judgments, not on the mores of the mob—will be the ones who succeed in the end, always.

—Robert B. Menschel

1

BOOMS, BUBBLES
& BUSTS

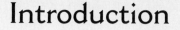 # Introduction

Stock markets seesaw between greed and fear. They always have, and they always will because the people whose decisions drive the markets seesaw between greed and fear themselves.

At the upper end of a market run, greed becomes what Federal Reserve Chairman Alan Greenspan once called "irrational exuberance"—a belief akin to faith that the curve is going to climb and climb and that whoever doesn't get aboard now is going to be forever left behind. Money comes pouring into the markets. The bubble grows and grows as old rules of valuation are tossed out the window along with almost all practical sense. Then comes the day of reckoning when the last fool is finally found. Fear reasserts itself. Irrational exuberance turns to flight, flight to panic, and panic maybe to outright disaster. The more air that has gone into the bubble, the faster it comes rushing out, and the deeper and steeper the fall.

All bubble markets share common trajectories, but as we'll explore in this section, each is unique in its own right. The tulipmania that swept Holland in the first part of the seventeenth century—the first of the modern bubble markets and even almost 400 years later still one of the most fascinating—wouldn't have been possible if the Dutch hadn't already invented the stock market. The stock market wouldn't have prospered if the Netherlands hadn't found itself suddenly awash with florins as the continent's lead-ing trading nation. And the price of tulip bulbs might never have been driven to such outlandish heights—as much as $110,000 in contemporary dollars for a single bulb—if newspapers hadn't been recently established to tout the virtues of the tulip and to remind readers that everyone was get-ting rich but them.

The two great runaway markets of the early eighteenth century—the South Sea Bubble in England and the Mississippi Bubble across the chan-nel in France—both involved stock companies set up, in theory, with patri-otic ends in mind. Both would bait the trap with seemingly exclusive access to the untapped resources of distant climes. Both at least initially produced staggering returns. Between January and August 1720, stock in the South Sea Company rose eightfold, to £1,000 a share. In France, shares in the Mississippi Company were sometimes doubling in value every 5 to 10 hours the market was open. And as happens with bubble markets, both col-lapsed as rapidly as they had risen, carrying under not just the wealthy but the poor and very nearly the national economy as well.

Like the South Sea and Mississippi Bubbles, the Florida land boom of the 1920s had an untapped resource to offer: acres and acres of newly platted land in a state only recently made accessible by railroad and by the new proliferation of cars and highways. The land boom had an untapped reservoir to work as well: the paper wealth created by the soar-ing stock market of the Roaring Twenties. Like all bubbles, too, the Florida one had no absence of scam artists and other con men ready to sell a parade of suckers building lots that proved to be swampland infested with alligators, snakes, and all the other creepy-crawly charms of Florida.

The granddaddy of all bubble market collapses, the one in October 1929 that ushered in the Great Depression, was itself inseparable from the rampant prosperity that had turned the 1920s into a charmed decade. Optimism was everywhere. So were easy money and margin accounts. Along the market roared—higher and higher until it reached the cliff that all bubble markets get to, and plunged straight down.

For its part, the recently deceased Internet market had just what bub-ble markets need: a new technology that seemed to be ushering in a new paradigm. Gone were the old bricks-and-mortar companies. From now on, businesses would be dematerialized, able to change directions on a dime and travel quick and light. Naturally, everyone bought into it. Even the financial houses that are supposed to be the stock markets' gatekeepers of common sense were bringing out new initial public offerings by the hour, it sometimes seemed, creating public stakes in companies that by the old standards barely existed. No wonder the crash came with such fury: There was almost no infrastructure to hold the bubble up, other than the hot air inside.

As distinct as each bubble market is, the psychology that drives investors is always essentially the same. Think back to the last high-tech stock you bought before the bottom fell out on Nasdaq. What information or impulse were you acting on? Maybe it was a tip from a good friend who is usually well informed. But where did he get his information? A newsletter? If so, what was the circulation? His broker? If so, how many other clients was his broker passing the same information on to? Inside dope is only inside for a second. Once it hits the street, the "inside" goes outside in an instant.

The other day I found myself wandering through the financial message boards on America Online to see where the crowds were gathering these days. Level 3 Communications had 235 postings on its board so I decided to drop in and have a look. A one-time favorite of the Street, Level 3 had been touted as maybe the leading builder of a nationwide fiber-optic network. Even after the April 2000 shakeout in tech stocks, its share price had held over $50, but by the midfall of 2001, Level 3 had hit a 52-week low of $1.89 and was sitting at $3.57. Losses for the third quarter of 2001 had been set at $437 million, up from a loss of $351 million for the third quarter of 2000. What would the messages say about this falling comet, I wondered? So I picked out a posting at random and had a look. Here's how it began:

"I have a friend who is a doctor who has invested a fair amount in Level 3 and who has invested more since listening to the third-quarter earnings conference call. He has studied this company and this stock for years and is convinced that this company will not only survive but will become a telecom leader after this shakeout."

Well, maybe it will, I thought. But when you look at secondhand information being passed on in an anonymous venue (screen names only are used, not real ones) and pegged to such a slim reed, you've got to think this guy is either a patsy, a shill, or just maybe a wise man. Problem is, there's no way to tell which.

We live, it is said, in the Information Age, but what is this information we live with? When it comes to the financial markets, so many people are in search of the hot tip, the one secret that will transform their luck forever that they are prey to every bill of goods that comes down the street. Play the numbers based on what some astrologer divines or what the tea leaves suggest? Never. But it's amazing to me still how many of us will play the stock market on not much more, driven by peer pressure, envy, and panic to find a shortcut that is, by its very nature, irrational in the extreme.

It's also amazing to me how, when these bubble markets fall apart as they always do, the media inevitably goes looking for the one precipitating event: the pinprick that began to let the air out. It's like children building a tower with blocks. Up goes one cockeyed story, then another and another, each more unstable than the last, until one tiny block seems to topple the whole thing. But it's not the block, it's not the event, it's not the collapse of a single stock that brings everything down. It's the instability built in at every step along the way. That's where you need to look: not at the top of the tower, but at the infrastructure that supports it, or fails to.

Here's what 40-plus years of investing my own money and my clients' money has taught me: There are plenty of wise men in this business, but there are no shortcuts to success, no end runs around due diligence, and no free lunches.

Looked at from the outside, Charles Ponzi had a wonderful idea. Beginning about 1920, his Boston-based Securities and Exchange Company (it predated the federal SEC) proposed to provide investors with incredible returns by exploiting the different exchange rates for International Postal Reply Coupons. Ponzi began by promising a 40 percent return in 90 days. Soon, his company was issuing 90-day notes at a 100-percent return and 45-day notes at 50 percent. To investors, the lure was irresistible. Ponzi's clerks were stacking banknotes in closets; wastebaskets were filled with dollar bills. The last fool, though, was finally found, as it always is, and the law caught on as well. Ponzi fled to Florida, where he tried his hand at real-estate fraud, and on to Rio de Janiero, where he died in a charity ward, but not before lending his name to the annals of crime.

Today, of course, Ponzi seems quaint. He was exploiting the Boston immigrant community; his scheme is transparent. And yet was Charles Ponzi's Securities and Exchange Company all that different from Reed Slatkin, the California investment adviser to whom some 800 wealthy people, including many Hollywood celebrities, entrusted nearly $600 million? Like Ponzi's company, Slatkin seemed to be manufacturing huge returns when, in fact, by Slatkin's own admission he was mostly manufacturing false earnings statements. Sometimes, the smarter or better known someone is, the more he seems willing to take nonsense on faith. Sometimes, too, the newer a con game appears the older it is.

Back in the early 1930s, Samuel Insull and his Middle West Utilities seemed like one of the few companies in a depression-ravaged economy that investors could still count on. Middle West had weathered the worst of the market collapse and come out well enough off for Insull to loan the city of Chicago $50 million to meet its payroll for teachers and police. A visionary as well as a good corporate citizen, Insull had advanced the then novel idea that central power plants should operate around the clock to help offset their high costs. To create demand for the increased supply, he pushed the idea of the "all-electric" home and even gave the language a new phrase for what he was proposing: "massing production," soon shortened to "mass production." It all worked great until 1934 when Middle West Utilities suddenly went bankrupt, exposing a long trail of crooked accounting practices, a huge pyramid of affiliates for hiding debt, and an avalanche of stock fraud that finally wiped out thousands of investors.

Substitute "Enron" for "Middle West Utilities," and you have pretty much the same story all over again: a groundbreaking approach to energy technology, a chief executive known for his large political donations and antipathy to federal regulation, a complex web of subsidiaries unknown to all but the most inside investors, and a trail of broken dreams for company employees and stockholders.

The collapse of Middle West Utilities shocked the political establishment: Within two years of its failure, Congress had passed the Securities and Exchange Act, the Public Utility Holding Company Act, and the Federal Power Act. So, too, the collapse of Enron shocked Washington. At hastily called hearings, members of Congress who only months earlier had been courting contributions from the company and heralding its innovative approach worked themselves into righteous indignation as they pilloried Enron chairman Kenneth Lay and other executives. Nor did the failure of Enron's accounting firm, Arthur Andersen, to run up a red flag go unnoticed. And yet, as always is the case with these blowups, the model was sitting out there all along. As columnist Paul Krugman wrote in the *New York Times,* "the most admired company in America turned out to have been a giant Ponzi scheme."

I have some specific investment strategies to suggest at the close of this chapter. Suffice it now to list three general principles that should help you avoid the Enrons of the future:

- The faster a stock has climbed, the quicker it will fall. In investing as in hare-and-tortoise races, slow and steady gets the prize.
- The easier information arrives, the less valuable it is. Good investment decisions are hard work, undertaken and arrived at one at a time.
- The more certain the crowd is, the surer it is to be wrong. If everyone were right, there would be no reward.

And a last truth as well: As it is with societies, so it is with investing— the price of freedom is eternal vigilance.

What can you count on then? Not the reports everyone else is reading, "everyone else" being the operative phrase. Not the newspaper and magazine articles touting 10 sure winners. (A magazine with a circulation of a million or more readers that seeks to provide "inside info" is absurd on the face of it.) Not the pundits or analysts either, unless you want to turn your brain over to someone whose agenda you can't possibly know. Inform yourself, of course. Read all you can. Listen to the latest geniuses. Field test your instincts constantly, but in the end, it comes down only to yourself, to the crowd of one. The babble will always be there; the crowd will always be roaring in one direction or another. Fear and greed will always be battling for the upper hand. But remember this above all else: When everybody else is doing it, don't.

*"Oh, I'm really sorry. I just placed three million with
some broker who called five minutes ago."*

~

*Markets as well as mobs respond to human emotions;
markets as well as mobs can be inflamed to their own
destruction.*

—Owen D. Young

The Bulb That Ate Holland:
Tulipmania

A market can be made in anything human beings are willing to buy and sell: stocks and bonds, currency, oil and gas, even sow bellies. All it takes is a collective willingness to trade risk and reward. By extension, a bubble market—one where the value of whatever is being traded comes unhinged from all reason—can be made in anything, too. In Holland, in the early part of the seventeenth century, the first of the great bubble markets was made in one of nature's more beautiful and unlikely items: tulips.

Some contributing factors have already been noted. The Dutch had practically invented the stock market only a few decades earlier, and expanded ocean trading had helped turn the maritime nation into Europe's greatest economic engine. Newspapers, too, had taken an early hold in Holland, and then as now, a commodity skyrocketing in value was a hard news story to ignore. A virulent outbreak of the bubonic plague had swept the nation, too, in 1635 and 1636, just as tulipmania was moving into high gear. One Dutch historian of the time—from Haarlem, a leading center of the tulip market—suggested in a postmortem to the madness that the sort of devil-may-care attitude that often follows mass death may have played a role as well:

"In the midst of all this misery that made our city suffer, people were caught by a special fever, by a particular anxiety to get rich in a very short period of time. The means to this were thought to be found in the tulip trade."

Sound like the "special fever" that seized investors in the Internet market bubble of the 1990s? It should. What began as an economic exchange between knowledgeable dealers in a very narrow and specific trading niche rapidly expanded to include buyers and sellers who had never been in the stock market before. A futures market of sorts was created. The commodity itself was split between high-priced, highly unique tulip stocks and low-priced common bulbs—the penny stocks of the early 1600s. And when the end came for this bubble market, too, it came with a roar. Providence University economist Peter Garber estimates that the price of a White Croonen tulip bulb soared 2,600 percent during January 1637, only to plummet by 95 percent in the first week of February.

In the mid-1630s, the prices of tulip bulbs soared to insane levels in Holland, but no bulb flew higher or crashed farther than that of the rare and beautiful Semper Augustus. In early 1637, just before the tulip bubble market broke, three Semper Augustus bulbs brought an offer of 30,000 florins, or roughly three times the value of a grand Amsterdam canal house.

In this essay, Barton Biggs, chief global strategist for Morgan Stanley Dean Witter, captures the spirit of madness that seems both peculiarly arcane and especially modern.

Tulips—so named it is said from the Turkish word signifying turban—were introduced into Western Europe from Turkey around 1550. The tulip becomes most beautiful when intensively cultivated and bred. But the more exquisite it becomes, the weaker and more fragile it grows so that only with great skill and most careful handling can it be cultivated. By the seventeenth century, tulips had become the fashion of the wealthy, especially in Germany and Holland. Prizes of increasingly large sums of money were given at competitions for the most beautiful bulbs. The winning bulbs could then be sold for cross breeding.

By 1630 the Dutch people in particular were becoming obsessed with the growing and trading of tulips. Amateur growers began to bid up the price of certain species that were especially popular or that had the potential of winning prizes, and by 1634 an adjunct to the Amsterdam stock exchange had been set up for the trading of tulips. The rage to own tulips became such that "persons were known to invest a fortune of 100,000 florins in the purchase of forty roots." Soon, everyone who had a few square yards of back garden was growing bulbs, and at first all were winners as the price of bulbs kept rising. Stories of common people cultivating rare bulbs and suddenly becoming rich abounded, and working men began to quit their jobs in order to have more time to grow and trade tulips.

As the new wealth swelled the money supply, the price of everything else began to rise also. In addition, money from England and other parts of Europe poured into Holland, and the Dutch imagined the passion for tulips would last forever and that the wealthy from every part of the world would buy Dutch tulips because they were uniquely beautiful. In the early days of the mania, sales took place between the end of June when the bulbs were taken out of the ground and September when they were replanted. But, as the fever increased, trading continued all year with delivery promised for the summer. As [the botanical illustrator] Wilfrid Blunt describes it:

"Thus a speculator often offered and paid large sums for a root which he never received, and never wished to receive. Another sold roots which he never possessed or delivered. Oft did a nobleman purchase of a chimney-sweep tulips to the amount of two-thousand florins, and sell them at the same time to a farmer; and neither the nobleman, chimney-sweep or farmer had roots in their possession, or wished to possess them. Before the tulip season was over, more roots were sold and purchased, bespoke and promised to be delivered than in all probability were to be found in the gardens of Holland."

The height of tulipmania was between 1634 and 1637. The price of prime bulbs soared to the present equivalent of $110,000. As the mania expanded, the fabric of society began to unravel. Farmers sold their livestock to raise capital to speculate in tulips, and houses and estates were mortgaged. No man's garden was safe from thieves, and in *The Black Tulip* there are tales of greed and depravity as the passions of the people became inflamed. Some growers only cultivated secret plots at night so rivals would not know of their stock. Visitors to Holland were astounded, and Charles Mackay [author of the classic study *Extraordinary Popular Delusions and the Madness of Crowds*] recounts the story of an ignorant English sailor off a visiting ship in Rotterdam happening to eat a tulip bulb from a garden, thinking it was an onion. Its owner turned out a lynch mob, and the sailor was committed to debtors prison for ten years. The craze spread to France and England by 1635, but most of the trading activity and wild speculation was centered in Holland.

In 1636 various coolheaded people warned of impending disaster and tried to restore the country's balance. One Evard Forstius, Professor of Botany at Leyden, could not see a tulip without attacking it with his walking stick. Eventually because of his anti-tulip harangues and attacks, he was judged criminally insane and committed to the dungeons. . . . Other notables cautioned of the consequences, but were mocked and derided.

The operations of the tulip trade became so intense and intricate that it was found necessary to create an entire infrastructure of notaries, clerks, and dealers. Tulip exchanges were established in many towns across the country. Normal trade and manufacture were neglected, and except for tulips, Dutch exports declined. But as long as prices stayed high it didn't matter, and in fact the Dutch people had never been so prosperous.

But the false prosperity couldn't last even though prices swept higher throughout 1635 and 1636. Suddenly, early in 1637 the crash came. . . . At first only a few people wanted to sell in order to convert their tulip holdings into other forms of wealth. No one wanted to buy. Prices declined 25%, and more sellers entered the market. In vain the dealers and exchanges resorted to such devices as mock auctions to build confidence, and new larger prizes were announced in the hope they would restore prices. Nothing worked, and suddenly prices really collapsed as sellers panicked. The value of prime bulbs such as

Semper Augustus, General Bol, and Admiral van Hoorn fell in a few weeks from 6,000 florins to 400 or 500 florins as it dawned on people that what they owned was bulbs and not real assets. As Mackay describes it:

"Hundreds who a few months previously had begun to doubt that there was such a thing as poverty in the land suddenly found

"I got out of tulips after the market collapsed, but I'm slowly getting back in. Especially pink ones."

themselves the possessors of a few bulbs which nobody would buy, even though they offered them at one quarter of the sums they had paid for them. The cry of distress sounded everywhere, and each man accused his neighbor. The few who had contrived to enrich themselves hid their wealth from the knowledge of their fellow citizens, and invested it in the English or other funds. Many who for a brief season had emerged from the humbler walks of life were cast back into their original obscurity. Substantial merchants were reduced almost to beggary, and many a representative of a noble line saw the fortunes of his house ruined beyond redemption."

Eventually, there were so many lawsuits filed that the courts could not handle them, and in April of 1637 the Court of Holland intervened in an effort to stabilize the social situation of the country. However, the court's complicated rulings were to no avail, and the sharp contraction of the wealth and money supply of the country caused a depression that lasted for some years.

∾

Nor is the people's judgment always true:
The most may err as grossly as the few.

—John Dryden

Booms & Bubbles

To become a player in a bubble stock market, you need nothing more than money to part with and a willingness to buy overpriced stock. To take part in the California gold rush that began with the discovery of some tiny nuggets at Sutter's Mill, along the American River in present-day Sacramento, you pretty much had to be there, and were they ever. Undeterred by formidable terrain and climate—not to mention hostile Native Americans—the get-rich-quick crowd stormed through the Great American Desert and across the Rocky Mountains and Sierra Nevadas. They came by sea as well. By July 1850, ghost ships crammed San Francisco harbor, abandoned by crews star-struck by tales of gold-lined streams in a state still largely wilderness. The U.S. Census of 1850 found fewer than 100,000 people living in California. By 1860, the population had grown fourfold.

A century and a half after the gold rush began, it's unlikely that most Americans would be able to name a single prospector who took part in it. Not so the people who supplied the miners.

For sturdy clothing that wouldn't fall apart in the rough mountains where the prospectors moiled for gold, they could turn to Levi Strauss, who used the gold rush to launch an eponymous clothing empire that persists, albeit rattled, to this day. For the shovels and picks and other tools that are so much a part of a prospector's lot, Collis Huntington was waiting. A one-time pushcart salesman, Huntington grew rich outfitting the forty-niners. But he didn't stop there. Along with Leland Stanford, Mark Hopkins, and Charles Crocker, he would be the principal backer of the Central Pacific Railroad, half of the transcontinental railroad that finally brought the nation together for good. In time, Huntington would branch into real estate, timber, coal mines, and real estate. At his death, he was said to be worth $70 million, but it all began with the hardware he sold to the prospectors, and therein lies the moral.

In booms, the sure money is more likely to be made by providing support services than by going after whatever has generated all the excitement in the first place. Michael Bloomberg was sitting on a trading desk when he realized that, while the stock market might offer great opportunities, being the best data provider for the marketplace offered even greater rewards. While others were chasing the top of such ultimate dotcom flameouts as Priceline and Doubleclick, Bloomberg was building a fortune that would help carry him to the New York City mayor's office.

Most towns barely survive one boom. Leadville, in the Colorado Rockies, has survived two: an 1860 gold rush, followed by a massive silver find in 1877 that turned tiny Leadville into a frontier cultural oasis, including an opera house that hosted Harry Houdini and Oscar Wilde, among others. This woodcut is from *Frank Leslie's Illustrated Newspaper* of April 12, 1879.

New Lands, New Schemes:
The South Sea
and Mississippi Companies

The power of greed alone is great enough to launch a stock-buying boom, but when you couple that power with unscrupulous and prominent men and with what appears to be the official approval of a national government, you have the stuff of which great bubble markets are made. So it was in the early 1700s, on either side of the English Channel.

In the United Kingdom, a series of European military campaigns led by the great Duke of Marlborough had been successfully concluded by the 1713 Peace of Utrecht. The postwar economic boom that followed turned the public's attention away from war to their own account books, and in the South Sea Company, they seemed to have found a perfect way to be patriotic while lining their own pockets. "Doing well by doing good," we might call it today—a call to conscience and country that is both noble and almost irresistible to con men.

In France, a crushing load of national debt spawned a similar mixing pot of greed and good intentions called the Mississippi Company. Both the South Sea and Mississippi Companies were to become involved in "exclusive trading rights" in distant lands, rights that had little practical worth yet still sparked the public imagination with dreams of unlimited wealth. Both seemed to promise a form of alchemy: They would make the national debt disappear at the same time they enriched everyone who invested. (A belief in alchemy is the lifeblood of such markets!) And because both seemingly unstoppable booms were going on simultaneously in nations that were virtual neighbors, even if longtime enemies, the critical mass of personal rapaciousness that bubble markets feed on grew and grew until there was only one way for fortunes to grow: straight down.

Here, in a pair of merged essays from his book *Contrary Investing*, Richard E. Band shows us how the bubbles grew and who was made to pay for them in the end.

Robert Harley, the Earl of Oxford, had founded the South Sea Company in 1711. The new company invited holders of £9 million worth of British government bonds to exchange their bonds for stock in the South Sea Company. For this patriotic service in retiring part of the national debt, the crown granted the South Sea Company a monopoly on British trade with the South Sea islands and South America.

As it turned out, the monopoly wasn't worth anywhere near as much as the earl had dreamed, because Spain, which ruled most of South America at the time, was unwilling to open its colonies to more than a trivial volume of British trade. But like all skillful corporate con artists before and since, Harley knew how to sell an enticing story to a gullible and greedy public. In 1720, the South Sea Company made Parliament an offer it couldn't refuse: The company would absorb virtually the entire national debt of £31 million by issuing South Sea stock to the bondholders.

Robert Walpole, later Britain's first prime minister, denounced the plan in the House of Commons, saying it was designed "to raise artificially the price of the stock, by exciting and keeping up a general infatuation, and by promising dividends out of funds which could never be adequate to the purpose." But Walpole's eloquence was powerless against the Earl of Oxford's rumor mill.

The earl's allies whispered that England and Spain were negotiating treaties that would concede to the English free trade with all the Spanish colonies. Gold and silver from the New World would flood into England, making the South Sea merchants the richest on earth. Every hundred pounds invested would return hundreds annually to the stockholder.

The bill passed, and the speculation began. From a price of £128-1/2 per share in January 1720, South Sea stock zoomed to a dizzying £1000 in August. Even Robert Walpole, who had spoken out against the scheme, couldn't resist. He, too, purchased a block of shares (and later lost heavily in the crash). People of all sorts and conditions joined the mad rush to get aboard the bull market.

It seemed at that time as if the whole nation had turned stockjobbers. Exchange Alley was every day blocked up by crowds, and Cornhill (a street in London's financial district) was impassable for the number of carriages. Everybody came to purchase stock.

The Bernie Cornfelds of the eighteenth century sensed an opportunity. Noticing how rapidly South Sea Company's shares were running up, swindlers formed hundreds of "bubble companies" that had little or no business purpose other than to peddle their own stock. One company was set up "for trading in hair." Another, which was trying to raise £1 million when it was outlawed, proposed to manufacture a perpetual-motion machine. A third was established "for the transmutation of quicksilver into a malleable fine metal." Since quicksilver, or mercury, is a liquid at any temperature above −38 degrees Fahrenheit, turning it into a solid metal would have been quite an accomplishment.

Perhaps the most remarkable scam was a company with no stated purpose at all. The prospectus coyly hinted that the company had been organized "for carrying on an undertaking of great advantage, but nobody to know what it is." For every £2 invested, the promoter declared that subscribers would be entitled to £100 a year in dividends—a 50 to 1 return. Dazzled by this unsubstantiated promise, a throng of people showed up at the entrepreneur's door the morning after the offering circular was published. In six hours, he collected £2000.

Having raked in a tidy sum for a day's work, the promoter, according to Charles Mackay, "was philosopher enough to be contented with his venture, and set off the same evening for the Continent. He was never heard of again."

Of course, we know that today the Securities and Exchange Commission would prevent such shady outfits from selling stock to the public. Right? At the height of the new-issues craze in June 1983, a twentieth-century bubble company announced on the front page of its prospectus, which was filed with the SEC:

"This offering is a securities of a start-up company with no operating history and no plan of operation: the company will not engage in any business whatever until after the completion of this offering."

On page 5, the prospectus further revealed: "The company does not know what business it will engage in, has no plan of operation. . . ." The wording bears a striking resemblance to the advertisement for the bubble company of 1720: "an undertaking of great advantage, but nobody to know what it is." Yet, amazingly, this modern bubble raised $3 million, at $5 per share. Two-and-a-half centuries later, a sucker is still being born every minute.

The South Sea bubble finally burst in August 1720, when news leaked out that the directors of the company—including the chairman, Sir John Blunt—had sold their stock. This vote of no confidence by the corporate insiders triggered a wave of panic selling that eventually drove the price of South Sea shares from £1000 at the peak to a low of only £315—a 68 percent decline. Thousands of English families were devastated financially, including many members of Parliament, and a general commercial depression settled over the land.

Not to be outdone, France had its own roaring speculative boom going on simultaneously with the South Sea Company madness across the English Channel.

The mastermind of the French fiasco was John Law, a flirtatious Scotsman who had fled to the Continent after killing his ladyfriend's lover in a duel. A compulsive gambler, Law was ideally equipped to launch one of history's most egregious flim-flams, the Mississippi Company.

In 1716, Law persuaded the French regent (who was ruling in place of the 6-year-old Louis XV) to allow him to set up a bank. At the time, France was deep in debt and the government had just devalued the coinage, reducing its gold and silver content. Law started out on the right foot. His bank issued paper money fully backed by precious metals, and—unlike the government—Law promised never to change the amount of metal standing behind each note. In fact, he declared that a banker deserved death if he issued notes without enough gold and silver on hand to make redemptions.

French citizens beat a path to his door. Within a year, Law's paper money was trading at a 15 percent premium to the government's coinage. Meanwhile, the government's unbacked paper currency, the billets d'état issued during the reign of Louis XIV, had fallen to an 80 percent discount from their nominal value in gold and silver.

Unfortunately, Law's gambling instinct got the better of him. At the regent's urging, he converted his bank into a royal (government) institution. With the blessing of the state, Law began to crank out vast quantities of paper money with no backing whatsoever. Interest rates fell and business picked up. An artificial inflationary boom was under way.

Law quickly hit upon a scheme to exploit the speculative atmosphere he had created. In 1717, the crown granted his Mississippi Company the exclusive right to trade up and down the Mississippi River, including the province of Louisiana, which belonged at the time to France. To attract buyers for the Mississippi Company's stock, Law promised a yearly dividend of 40 percent—an incredible return by the standards of any era.

But Law went a step further. As a favor to his patron who was trying to reduce the national debt, Law told investors they could pay for their subscriptions with the government's next-to-worthless billets d'état. Since the dividend was to be paid in real money (gold or silver coin), Law was in effect promising that shareholders could earn a 120 percent annual yield on their investment from dividends alone.

"The public enthusiasm," Charles Mackay writes, "which had been so long rising, could not resist a vision so splendid." Dukes, marquis, and counts—together with their wives—besieged Law with applications to buy shares. Each new issue was a sellout, even after Law upped the price tenfold! The rue de Quincampoix in Paris, where the great man had his office, was jammed with speculators buying and selling Mississippi Company shares.

As the trading reached a fever pitch, share prices sometimes rose 10 to 20 percent in a few hours—a scene reminiscent of the last days of the 1929 stock market boom. Maids and footmen parlayed their meager savings into instant fortunes. Mackay relates that "many persons in the humbler walks of life, who had risen poor in the morning, went to bed in affluence."

Fueled by fiat money, the artificial boom spread from the rue de Quincampoix across Paris and into the hinterlands. Inflation ran wild, with prices spiraling 300 percent in the space of a few months. Luxury goods rose especially fast as successful speculators channeled their profits into hard assets:

"The looms of the country worked with unusual activity to supply rich laces, silks, broad-cloth and velvets, which being paid for in abundant paper, increased in price fourfold. . . . New houses were built in every direction: an illusory prosperity shone over the land, and so dazzled the eyes of the whole nation, that none could see the dark cloud on the horizon announcing the storm that was too rapidly approaching."

Early in 1720, the first cracks began to appear in Law's magnificent structure. A leading nobleman, the Prince de Conti, caused a stir when he brought three wagons full of paper money to Law's bank and demanded payment in specie, or metal. The regent browbeat the prince into returning two-thirds of his withdrawal to the bank, but the con game was up. Aware that the banknotes were losing their purchasing power daily, people hurried to cash them in for gold and silver.

However, there wasn't enough specie in Law's bank to satisfy the demand. A run on the bank ensued, together with a disastrous collapse in the price of Mississippi Company stock. Although the government tried to restore confidence in the currency by devaluing gold and silver in terms of paper money, nobody fell for the ruse. The panic only intensified. As a final expedient, the tyrannical regent forbade private citizens to possess more than a token amount of gold and silver.

In a last-ditch effort to prop up the Mississippi Company's stock, Law asked the government to conscript 6,000 Parisian street urchins to work the supposedly abundant gold mines in Louisiana. Law paraded these derelicts through Paris with picks and shovels, convincing a few naive investors that his scheme still had merit.

The price of the stock took a brief bounce—hope springs eternal—but then, as the effects of Law's public-relations stunt wore off, quotations began to slide once more. Mississippi Company shares, which had soared from 500 livres apiece in 1716 to 20,000 livres at the peak in 1720, plunged within a few months to only 200 livres, a staggering 99 percent loss. Law was ruined, and so—very nearly—was the French economy.

Run on a bank, from *Harper's Magazine*, February 1890. The economist John Kenneth Galbraith once noted that Americans endured a bank panic roughly every 20 years during the nineteenth century—just about the time it took them to forget the last one.

~

It is an easy and vulgar thing to please the mob, and no very arduous task to astonish them.

—Charles Caleb Colton

Panics & Runs

Stock market collapses are, in a sense, impersonal. A share of stock is nothing more than a fractional ownership in the entity that has issued it. Its value is either what someone else is willing to give you for it, or the fraction of interest it represents should the entity cease to exist as a public company. Either way, the monetary value of the share is third party at best. Bank collapses are more personal because the bank is the custodian of our ready cash. When those doors start shuttering up, the real panic sets in and the run is on. In a rising bubble market the last fool to buy is the one who usually gets stuck with the biggest loss. In a bank panic, the last fool in line is the one least likely to regain his assets.

The nineteenth century provided two notable examples of the hysteria that sets in when banking institutions begin to teeter and fall. The economic boom that swept the victorious North after the close of the Civil War was cut short by the panic of 1873. Twenty years later, just as things were settling down again, along came the panic of 1893 to send deposit holders scurrying to the bank doors.

In the first instance, the panic was brought on by the failure of a leading Philadelphia bank, Jay Cooke and Company, and the subsequent fear that other banks were going to fall like dominoes. The 1893 panic had a more specific thermometer at hand. Collective wisdom held that the federal treasury needed to hold $100 million in reserves to assure government obligations could be redeemed in gold. When the number dipped below $100 million on April 21, 1893, collective wisdom suddenly held that the end was near. In both cases, the panics were exaggerated by the absence of any real central banking authority—and given added urgency, too, by the fact that deposits weren't federally insured then as they are today.

But if America lacked a central banking system, it didn't lack a central banker: J. Pierpont Morgan, whose life almost perfectly fills the space between Andrew Jackson's abolition of the United States Bank in 1837 and the creation of the Federal Reserve System in 1913. In 1873, Morgan was the central mover in the creation of a bond issue that replenished depleted federal coffers and restored public confidence enough for banks to get back on their feet. Two decades later, Morgan looked at the federal balance sheet, saw that the treasury was $62 million short of the panic

In 1948, as it prepared to flee mainland China for Taiwan, the Nationalist government, or *Kuomintang,* issued an order requiring all individuals to exchange their gold, silver, and foreign monies for a new currency, the *Jingyuanquan.* A few months later, the *Kuomintang* reversed its policy. In this Henri Cartier-Bresson photo, residents of Shanghai line up to buy gold during the last days of *Kuomintang* rule.

mark of $100 million, and loaned the government the $62 million in gold—at, of course, not unfavorable terms to himself in either case.

"Wars and panics on the stock exchange, bankruptcies, warloans, good growing weather for the House of Morgan." Thus wrote John Dos Passos in his *U.S.A.* trilogy, and thus it has always been for those who can keep their heads, and their purses, in the midst of seeming financial catastrophe.

～

Panics sometimes have their uses. Their duration is usually short and the mind soon grows through them and acquires a firmer habit.

—Thomas Paine

Crash: The Great Depression

When stock market bubbles break, paper wealth is lost in the billions and sometimes trillions. When banks fail, real wealth disappears or, in these days of insured deposits, is at least delayed. When both happen simultaneously and when that failure is repeated on a global scale, a Great Depression is on.

History books tell us that the stock market crash came on Black Thursday, October 24, 1929, and it's true that $4 billion in paper worth disappeared on that day alone and that many accounts and many investors with them were wiped out, never to recover. But nothing as complex as a Great Depression happens at a single stroke.

As early as the spring of 1927, the Bank of England lowered interest rates in an effort to boost sagging British industries. Not surprisingly, gold soon began to flee England for America, in search of better returns. To put a brake on the outflow, the governor of the Bank of England convinced the Federal Reserve Board to lower interest rates in the United States, too, and with that an inflationary cycle was launched that would lead in a furious beeline to an orgy of stock speculation. From a 1927 low of 153, the Dow Jones Industrial Average would soar to a high of 381 in October 1929—a climb of nearly 250 percent in a scant two years.

Native character and a good deal of boosterism didn't hurt either. A 1929 commission on the economy appointed by President Calvin Coolidge and including, among others, soon-to-be-president Herbert Hoover, declared, "We seem only to have touched the fringe of our potentialities." And the Republicans weren't alone. Al Smith, the "Happy Warrior" Democratic governor of New York, whom Hoover defeated in the election of 1928, liked to say that "The American people never carry an umbrella, they prepare to walk in eternal sunshine." An August 1929 book by one Amos Dice, titled *New Levels in the Stockmarket,* is typical of the attitude:

· Our whole history tends to make us optimists. We have seen our country as it has grown at a tremendous rate in population; in wealth; and in the desire for the finer things. Each generation has been thrilled by the rapidity of the progress which it has experienced in its lifetime. An optimistic psychology is in the very air.

On October 24, 1929, all these forces collided with the reality that stock prices once again had lost all touch with value, but this time in a world that still hadn't settled the war that had rocked the end of the previous decade. Just as important, investors were dangerously overexposed. The great innovation of the closing years of the bubble market of the 1920s had been leverage. Margin accounts mushroomed as speculators borrowed at low interest rates. Today, investors have to put up 50 percent to borrow on margin; then, they needed to put up only 5 percent. In effect, even small-time players could make their own arrangements. On Black Thursday the bill for such massive carelessness finally came due.

Five days after the crash, the *New York Times* editorialized as follows, emboldened by hindsight but right all the same:

> On the stock market itself there is little need for moralizing. It has told its own story, and taught its own lessons. Of the extraordinary illusions concerning finance, economics and prosperity, which for two years have been defended and encouraged by men whose position gave small excuse for such an attitude it is not necessary now to speak. These intellectual vagaries, too, have gone down with the Wall Street Storm.

The first-person account of Black Thursday that follows, by Elliott V. Bell, is taken from a 1938 collection of essays titled *We Saw It Happen*. At the time of the crash, Bell was a reporter for the *New York Times*. He would later become editor and publisher of *Business Week*.

October 24, 1929, was not the first day of the big break in stocks, nor was it the last. Nevertheless, it was the most terrifying and unreal day I have ever seen on the Street, and it constitutes an important financial landmark, for that day marked the great decline in the prestige and power of Wall Street over national affairs.

The day was overcast and cool. A light north-west wind blew down the canyons of Wall Street, and the temperature, in the low fifties, made bankers and brokers on their way to work button their topcoats around them. The crowds of market traders in the brokers' board rooms were nervous but hopeful as the ten o'clock hour for the start of trading approached. The general feeling was that the worst was over and a good many speculators who had prudently sold out earlier in the decline were congratulating themselves at having bought back their stocks a good deal cheaper. Seldom had the small trader had better or more uniform advice to go by.

The market opened steady with prices little changed from the previous day, though some rather large blocks, of 20,000 to 25,000 shares, came out at the start. It sagged easily for the first half-hour, and then around eleven o'clock the deluge broke.

It came with a speed and ferocity that left men dazed. The bottom simply fell out of the market. From all over the country a torrent of selling orders poured onto the floor of the Stock Exchange and there were no buying orders to meet it. Quotations of representative active issues, like Steel [U.S. Steel], Telephone [AT&T], and Anaconda, began to fall two, three, five, and even ten points between sales. Less active stocks became unmarketable. Within a few moments the ticker service was hopelessly swamped and from then on no one knew what was really happening. By one-thirty the ticker tape was nearly two hours late; by two-thirty it was 147 minutes late. The last quotation was not printed on the tape until 7:08½ p.m., four hours, eight and one-half minutes after the close. In the meantime, Wall Street had lived through an incredible nightmare.

In the strange way that news of a disaster spreads, the word of the market collapse flashed through the city. By noon great crowds had gathered at the corner of Broad and Wall streets where the Stock Exchange on one corner faces Morgan's across the way. On the steps of the Sub-Treasury Building, opposite Morgan's, a crowd of press photographers and newsreel men took up their stand. Traffic was pushed from the streets of the financial district by the crush.

It was in this wild setting that the leading bankers scurried into conference at Morgan's in a belated effort to save the day. Shortly after noon Mr. [Charles E.] Mitchell left the National City Bank and pushed his way west on Wall Street to Morgan's. No sooner had he entered than Albert H. Wiggin was seen to hurry down from the Chase National Bank, one block north. Hard on his heels came William C. Potter, head of the Guaranty Trust, followed by Seward

Prosser of the Bankers Trust. Later George F. Baker, Jr., of the First National, joined the group.

The news of the bankers' meeting flashed through the streets and over the news tickers—stocks began to rally—but for many it was already too late. Thousands of traders, little and big, had gone "overboard" in that incredible hour between eleven and twelve. Confidence in the financial and political leaders of the country, faith in the "soundness" of economic conditions had received a shattering blow. The panic was on.

At Morgan's the heads of six banks formed a consortium since known as the bankers' pool of October 1929—pledging a total of $240,000,000, or $40,000,000 each, to provide a "cushion" of buying power beneath the falling market. In addition, other financial institutions, including James Speyer and Company and Guggenheim Brothers, sent over to Morgan's unsolicited offers of funds aggregating $100,000,000. It was not only the first authenticated instance of a bankers' pool in stocks but by far the largest concentration of pool buying power ever brought to bear on the stock market—but in the face of the panic it was pitifully inadequate.

After the bankers had met, Thomas W. Lamont, Morgan's partner, came out to the crowd of newspaper reporters who had gathered in the lobby of his bank. In an understatement that has since become a Wall Street classic, he remarked:

"It seems there has been some disturbed selling in the market."

It was at the same meeting that "T.W." gave to the financial community a new phrase—"air pockets," to describe the condition in stocks for which there were no bids, but only frantic offers. (Mr. Lamont said he had it from his partner, George Whitney, and the latter said he had it from some broker.)

After the meeting, Mr. Lamont walked across Broad Street to the Stock Exchange to meet with the governors of the Exchange. They had been called together quietly during trading hours and they held their meeting in the rooms of the Stock Clearing Corporation so as to avoid attracting attention. Mr. Lamont sat on the corner of a desk and told them about the pool. Then he said:

"Gentlemen, there is no man nor group of men who can buy all the stocks that the American public can sell."

It seems a pretty obvious statement now, but it had a horrid sound to the assembled governors of the Exchange. It meant that the shrewdest member of the most powerful banking house in the country was telling them plainly that the assembled resources of Wall Street, mobilized on a scale never before attempted, could not stop this panic.

The bankers' pool, in fact, turned out a sorry fiasco. Without it, no doubt, the Exchange would have been forced to close, for it did supply bids at some price for the so-called pivotal stocks when, because of the panic and confusion in the market, there were no other bids available. It made a small profit, but it did not have a ghost of a chance of stemming the avalanche of selling that poured in from all over the country. The stock market had become too big. The days that followed are blurred in retrospect. Wall Street became a nightmarish spectacle.

The animal roar that rises from the floor of the Stock Exchange and which on active days is plainly audible in the Street outside, became louder, anguished, terrifying. The streets were crammed with a mixed crowd—agonized little speculators, walking aimlessly outdoors because they feared to face the ticker and the margin clerk; sold-out traders, morbidly impelled to visit the scene of their ruin; inquisitive individuals and tourists, seeking by gazing at the exteriors of the Exchange and the big banks to get a closer view of the national catastrophe; runners, frantically pushing their way through the throng of idle and curious in their effort to make deliveries of the unprecedented volume of securities which was being traded on the floor of the Exchange.

The ticker, hopelessly swamped, fell hours behind the actual trading and became completely meaningless. Far into the night, and often all night long, the lights blazed in the windows of the tall office buildings where margin clerks and bookkeepers struggled with the desperate task of trying to clear one day's business before the next began. They fainted at their desks; the weary runners fell exhausted on the

On October 24, 1929, the bubble market that had been building throughout the late 1920s finally burst, launching the Great Depression. Here, panicked stock traders swarm in front of the New York Stock Exchange as the paper losses mount into the billions. (© Bettmann/CORBIS)

marble floors of banks and slept. But within a few months they were to have ample time to rest up. By then thousands of them had been fired.

Agonizing scenes were enacted in the customers' rooms of the various brokers. There, traders who a few short days before had luxuriated in delusions of wealth saw all their hopes smashed in a collapse so devastating, so far beyond their wildest fears, as to seem unreal. Seeking to save a little from the wreckage, they would order their stocks sold "at the market," in many cases to discover that they had not merely lost everything but were, in addition, in debt to the broker. And then, ironic twist, as like as not the next few hours' wild churning of the market would lift prices to levels where they might have sold out and had a substantial cash balance left over. Every move was wrong in those days. The market seemed like an insensate thing that was wreaking a wild and pitiless revenge upon those who had thought to master it.

The excitement and sense of danger which imbued Wall Street was like that which grips men on a sinking ship. A camaraderie, a kind of gaiety of despair, sprang up. The Wall Street reporter found all doors open and everyone snatched at him for the latest news, for shreds of rumor. Who was in trouble? Who had gone under last? Where was it going to end?

I remember dropping in to see a vice-president of one of the larger banks. He was walking back and forth in his office.

"Well, Elliott," he said, "I thought I was a millionaire a few days ago—Now I find I'm looking through the wrong end of the telescope."

He laughed. Then he said: "We'll get those bastards that did this yet."

∽

Men have been swindled by other men on many occasions. The autumn of 1929 was, perhaps, the first occasion when men succeeded on a large scale in swindling themselves.

—John Kenneth Galbraith

He Said/She Said

How easy is it for a small investor to get reliable information during a market frenzy? Readers will have their own memories from the Internet run-up, but investors were just as whipsawed back in 1929 before and during the great crash, as shown by this collection of headlines from the *New York Times*. The ever-optimistic "Fisher" referred to in several headlines is Irving Fisher, a Yale professor and leading market commentator of the day who also doubled as director of an investment company.

(Wednesday, July 3, 1929, Page 31)
SEES STOCK RISE JUSTIFIED
Moody's Says Returns Are In Line With Industrial Activity

(Friday, September 6, 1929, Page 12)
BABSON PREDICTS "CRASH" IN STOCKS
Says Wise Investors Will Pay Up Loans And Avoid Margin Trading

(Sunday, October 6, 1929, Page 1)
BRISK RALLY CHECKS LONG MARKET DROP; STOCKS RISE SHARPLY

(Sunday, October 13, 1929, Section 2, Page 7)
STOCK PRICES WILL STAY AT HIGH LEVEL FOR YEARS TO COME, SAYS OHIO ECONOMIST

(Wednesday, October 16, 1929, Page 8)
FISHER SEES STOCKS PERMANENTLY HIGH
Yale Economist Tells Purchasing Agents Increased Earnings Justify Rise
(Page 41)
MITCHELL ASSERTS STOCKS ARE SOUND
Banker, Sailing from Europe, Says He Sees No Signs of Wall Street Slump

(Sunday, October 20, 1929, Page 1)
STOCKS DRIVEN DOWN AS WAVE OF SELLING ENGULFS THE MARKET

(Tuesday, October 22, 1929, Page 24)
FISHER SAYS PRICES OF STOCKS ARE LOW
Quotations Have Not Caught Up With Real Values As Yet, He Declares

WASHINGTON VIEWS SITUATION AS SOUND
Officials Hold That Decline in Stocks Will Not Disturb Business Materially

(Wednesday, October 23, 1929, Page 1)
STOCKS GAIN SHARPLY BUT SLIP NEAR CLOSE
Vigorous Recovery Marks Most of Day and Many Issues Show Net Advances

MARKET GLOOM LESSENED
Banking Support, Ease of Money and Mitchell's Optimistic Statement Help Rally

(Thursday, October 24, 1929, Page 1)
PRICES OF STOCKS CRASH IN HEAVY LIQUIDATION, TOTAL DROP OF BILLIONS
PAPER LOSS $4,000,000,000
2,600,000 Shares Sold In The Final Hour In Record Decline

(Page 2)
SAYS STOCK SLUMP IS ONLY TEMPORARY
Professor Fisher Tells Capital Bankers Market Rise Since War Has Been Justified

ECONOMIC REASONS CITED
"Public Speculative Mania," He Declares, Is Least Important Cause of Price Inflation

(Friday, October 25, 1929, Page 1)
WORST STOCK CRASH STEMMED BY BANKS;
12,894,650-SHARE DAY SWAMPS MARKET;
LEADERS CONFER, FIND CONDITIONS SOUND

WALL STREET OPTIMISTIC AFTER STORMY DAY;
CLERICAL WORK MAY FORCE HOLIDAY TOMORROW

(Saturday, October 26, 1929, Page 1)
STOCKS GAIN AS MARKET IS STEADIED;
BANKERS PLEDGE CONTINUED SUPPORT;
HOOVER SAYS BUSINESS BASIS IS SOUND

(Tuesday, October 29, 1929, Page 1)
**STOCK PRICES SLUMP $14,000,000,000
IN NATION-WIDE STAMPEDE TO UNLOAD;
BANKERS TO SUPPORT MARKET TODAY**

(Wednesday, October 30, 1929, Page 1)
**STOCKS COLLAPSE IN 16,410,030-SHARE DAY,
BUT RALLY AT CLOSE CHEERS BROKERS;
BANKERS OPTIMISTIC, TO CONTINUE AID**
Closing Rally Vigorous

(Friday, November 1, 1929, Page 3)
SISSON DECRIES INFLATION
Lays Crash to Small Investors' Lack of Experience

(Thursday, December 19, 1929, Page 36)
LAYS STOCK BREAKS TO MOB PSYCHOLOGY
*W.W. Price Says Crashes Will Come So Long as Facilities for
Speculation Exist*

Bernard Baruch on Basic Math
& Eternal Truths

The financier Bernard Baruch made his own fortune in speculative stocks and used that fortune and a vast intellect to leverage himself into public life as an adviser to presidents, including the chairmanship of the War Industries Board during World War I and a seat on the postwar Supreme Economic Council at the Versailles peace talks.

As the 1930s broke, though, Baruch had had enough of stock speculation and mob psychology. With his own money, he paid to reprint and distribute a pamphlet that had been popular in Holland after the collapse of the tulip market, warning investors of getting caught up in the frenzy of the crowd and advising as well that they look to more stable companies and commodities. (The pamphlet had been paid for originally by some of the low-return stock companies that had been ignored during tulipmania.) Baruch also wrote this introduction to a 1934 edition of Charles Mackay's *Extraordinary Popular Delusions and the Madness of Crowds,* first published in 1841.

All economic movements, by their very nature, are motivated by crowd psychology. Graphs and business ratios are, of course, indispensable in our groping efforts to find dependable rules to guide us in our present world of alarms. Yet I never see a brilliant economic thesis expounding, as though they were geometrical theorems, the mathematics of price movements, that I do not recall Schiller's dictum: Anyone taken as an individual is tolerably sensible and reasonable—as a member of a crowd, he at once becomes a blockhead; or Napoleon's maxim about military masses: "In war, the moral is to the physical as 3 to 1." Without due recognition of crowd-thinking (which often seems crowd-madness) our theories of economics leave much to be desired. It is a force wholly impalpable—perhaps little amenable to analysis and less to guidance—and yet, knowledge of it is necessary to right judgments on passing events.

A proponent of a great organized mass movement, otherwise not very logical, recently sought to justify it by this colloquy: "Have you ever seen, in some wood, on a sunny quiet day, a cloud of flying midges—thousands of them—hovering, apparently motionless, in a sunbeam? ... Yes? ... Well, did you ever see the whole flight—each mite apparently preserving its distance from all others—suddenly move, say three feet, to one side or the other? Well, what made them do that? A breeze? I said a quiet day. But try to recall—did you ever see them move directly back again in the same unison? Well, what made them do that? Great human mass movements are slower of inception but much more effective."

Entomologists may be able to answer the question about the midges and to say what force creates such unitary movement by thousands of individuals, but I have never seen the answer. The migration of some types of birds; the incredible mass performance of the whole species of ocean eels; the prehistoric tribal human eruptions from Central Asia; the Crusades; the mediaeval dance crazes; or, getting closer to economics, the Mississippi and South Sea Bubbles; the Tulip Craze; and (are we too close to add?) the Florida boom and the 1929 market-madness in America and its sequences in 1930 and 1931—all these are phenomena of mass action under impulsions and controls which no science has explored. They have power unexpectedly to affect any static condition or so-called normal trend. For that reason, they have place in the considerations of thoughtful students of world economic conditions. ...

Although there be no scientific cure, yet, as in all primitive, unknown (and therefore diabolic) spells, there may be potent incantations. I have always thought that if, in the lamentable era of the "New Economics," culminating in 1929, even in the very presence of dizzily spiralling prices, we had all continuously repeated, "two and two still make four," much of the evil might have been averted. Similarly, even in the general moment of gloom in which this foreword is written, when many begin to wonder if declines will never halt, the appropriate abracadabra may be: "They always did."

～

The more intense the craze, the higher the type of intellect that succumbs to it.

—Benjamin Anderson,
Economics and the Public Welfare

Doonesbury

BY GARRY TRUDEAU

The four most expensive words in the English language are "this time it's different."

—John Templeton

Making the Play: The Internet and the "New" Economy

Whether it's tulip bulbs, "exclusive" trading rights, or "dematerialized" businesses that enflame the public imagination, all stock-market bubbles have a common denominator: Money, it suddenly dawns on everyone, is easy to make. Getting rich is a game! In his wonderful anecdotal history of the 1920s, *Only Yesterday*, Frederick Lewis Allen captures the spirit of the months before the great crash of 1929:

> The rich man's chauffeur drove with his ear laid back to catch the news of an impending move in Bethlehem Steel; he held fifty shares himself on a twenty-point margin. The window-cleaner at the broker's office paused to watch the ticker, for he was thinking of converting his laboriously accumulated savings into a few shares of Simmons. [Reporter] Edwin Lefevre told of a broker's valet who had made nearly a quarter of a million in the market, of a trained nurse who cleaned up thirty thousand following the tips given her by grateful clients; and of a Wyoming cattleman, thirty miles from the nearest railroad, who bought or sold a thousand shares a day. . . . Thousands speculated—and won, too—without the slightest knowledge of the nature of the company upon whose fortunes they were relying.

Six decades later, *Forbes* magazine, the self-proclaimed "capitalist tool," was telling essentially the same stories about a different market still driven by the eternal human desire to make a bundle with the least work possible. *Forbes* wrote in its January 25, 1999, issue:

> Each day a 5-million strong mob of online investors is proving that, when it comes to stock picking, might makes right. In their world, everything you have learned about rational pricing—earnings or book value or even revenues—is meaningless. Don't worry about the long haul. Trade for the moment. Make a killing. Hey, everyone else in the chat room seems to be doing so.

One personal injury lawyer told *Forbes,* "I cannot wait to get up in the morning and trade. This is the most exciting thing in the world for me right now. My philosophy is to buy high and sell higher and not be afraid to take risks. I use no research tools or software; I just surf the message boards and look for volume."

We know how this story ended, too. Thanks to Michael Lewis's book *Next,* we also know about the New Jersey teenager who manipulated those message boards and chat rooms to enrich himself by several hundred thousands of dollars. The Securities and Exchange Commission finally caught up with the boy, but give him credit. Although he was barely in high school, he already had a Ph.D.-level understanding of greed and the psychology of the mob.

The following, appropriately, is abridged from FrontPageMagazine.com, one of many 'zines (or dematerialized magazines) that sprang up to serve the Internet boom. The author, Robert Locke, was a computer company executive during the height of the boom. Writing in April 2001, a year after the bottom fell out on high-tech stocks, Locke is still close enough to the moment, and the pain, to feel both anger and feistiness.

The key to the new economy fantasy was the mutual reinforcement of stupid ideas by stupid money. Stupid money is money that gets made without hard work. No one but a red has a problem with stock-market speculation as such, but when people make money investing in peanutbuttersandwiches.com despite the fact that the company is going broke, it does have the unfortunate consequence of validating whatever dumb logic led them to the investment. At the height of the boom, anyone who questioned the proposition that we were witnessing the emergence of something fundamental enough to be called a whole new economy was derided with the taunt, "You be right, and I'll be rich." This was quite stinging in a world where the fundamental profitability of many dot-companies was totally irrelevant to whether they made money for their investors. The creepy thing, of course, is that this argument concedes that the fundamental economic logic is against it. It just doesn't care, and the scary thing is that it doesn't have to. But fundamentals are, of course, never irrelevant, and having a stock market that makes people think they are is a recipe for disaster in the long run.

The most dangerous words in the English language are "it's different this time." A speculative boom in the stock market can't change the basic laws of business, like the idea that companies have to make a profit, but it can, dangerously, make people believe that they have changed. We have had speculative booms before, most famously in the 1920s, and they, too, had their rationalizations about how technology had changed everything. In the '20s, the hot technologies were radio, automobiles, and aviation. They still crashed. . . .

The other problem that surfaced in the recent boom is the ability of capitalism to bribe itself. In ideal capitalism, corporations respond to economic signals contained in prices as rational economic actors. Their Achilles heel is that they aren't really economic actors in their own right, but giant social machines piloted by fallible human beings. So what if the interests of management were not the same as that of the companies they run? Well, giving stock options to management can bring this about, because it means that generating a run-up in the stock price becomes the highest goal of management, a goal that can be more easily served by verbally positioning the company as a "new economy stock" than by actually making profits. And in a generalized stock-market boom, any fool running a company looks like a hero. . . .

Let no one misunderstand: there is nothing fundamentally wrong with the Internet and associated technologies as tools for doing business. They are very useful for a lot of things. They do a lot of things better than the old ways, and a lot of people are obviously going to make a lot of money doing this. But somehow this got inflated into the idea that "the Net changes everything." Basically people believed this not because they misinterpreted any specific facts, but because they emotionally wanted to. There were three reasons for this:

1. When people see other people getting rich, and get told that they can get rich too if they will only believe the same things as those who got there first, guess what they'll do?
2. The counter-culture invaded Silicon Valley. Baby-boomers have a huge unfulfilled longing from their formative years for

revolution. They have also learned the pleasures of wealth since then. The idea that the Internet constituted a revolution gave them both at once. The other thing the counter-culture did was it made technology hip. Think back to the last technology boom, in the 80's. Technology was popular, but it was never culturally hip. This time it was, which was lots of fun for the nerds who never dreamed they would be considered hip, but had the disastrous effect of making people totally incapable of being objective about technology.

3. Globalists tried to use the Internet as an intellectual bludgeon to argue that globalism was inevitable. Their favorite argument was (and is) that high technology just dictates globalism and there is nothing anyone can do about it. . . .

Globalists argued first the (utterly absurd) line that the Net made physical place irrelevant, which carries the tacit implication that national borders are obsolete. They then conjured up a vague but dazzling vision of a futuristic world in which everything is so different that all merely traditional values are obsolete. Technology people are extremely naive about politics and easily sold on any agenda that gives them an exalted place in its theology. The globalist ideologues (most of whom don't really know much about technology) are suckers for the most preposterous projections of what technology will do, so they bring out the worst in each other perfectly.

The really dangerous thing about the cultural argument is that when made explicit, it became identical with the idea that anyone who didn't believe the fantasy "just didn't get it" and was therefore not worth listening to despite the logic of anything they might say. It's oddly like a religious sect where any criticism simply shows that the critic is not among the saved. This made the hype-world of the boom hermetic against criticism. These nerds have been living in a world apart for decades, anyway, and the idea that they were heroes of an irresistible future that outsiders couldn't understand was pure mind-candy for them. How could they resist it?

The dot-com crash has also revealed flaws in the new hero of the 90's: the entrepreneur. The basic problem with entrepreneurs is that

because their companies are not just businesses to them but their principal creative expression in life, they have great difficulty being objective about them. Irrational faith in a great idea that the world doesn't recognize may be a good thing, but entrepreneurs also have irrational faith in dumb ideas simply because they are their own companies. They also have a suspicious love of being visionaries with other people's money. Most successful entrepreneurs are not vision-aries anyway, just ordinary competent businessmen, but in the boom, they were all expected to become visionaries, leading to an artificial love of radical business ideas for their own sake. ...

The sad thing is that a lot of Internet companies didn't have to fail, but blew their chances through arrogance and stupidity, attitudes that were encouraged by the boom atmosphere. For example, one buyproduce.com tried to create a wholesale online produce exchange. It sounded like a can't-lose idea, given how efficient the web is at link-ing people all around the world. But they had great difficulty getting wholesalers to sign up. Why? Because their system wasn't designed to cope with the fact that canceled orders in the produce business don't just disappear, but do various other things. Or with the simple fact that different wholesalers have different codes for the various colors that vegetables come in! Now how hard would these requirements have been to learn if they had just done their basic homework? Not very. But if you hew to the philosophy that "the Internet changes everything," then there's no need to do your homework. Your idea is so brilliant that it is guaranteed to make money and mere execution details aren't that important. And of course there's certainly no need to take seriously the old ways of doing things. You should assume, instead, that a multi-billion dollar industry in the mid-1990s was doing everything wrong until you came along. It is a time-honored lesson of history that arrogance is a sign one is in trouble; it was right once again.

The even more revealing thing about this particular company is that produce wholesalers apparently eventually concluded that the humble telephone and fax machine would give them everything they wanted, and without paying a transaction fee. People have in their heads the tacit idea that the more advanced the technology, the more productive it will be. This just isn't so. What's productive, and what isn't, are empirical questions, to be found out by experience, not deduced out of thin air. People have just got to get it into their thick heads that higher-tech isn't always better. A helicopter may not be the best way to deliver groceries.

~

And what the people but a herd confused,
A miscellaneous rabble, who extol
Things vulgar, and well weigh'd, scarce worth the
    praise?
They praise and they admire they know not what,
And know not whom, but as one leads the other.
           —John Milton, *Paradise Regained*

A Bubble Is a Bubble Is a Bubble

Every bubble market is different, and every bubble market is exactly alike. Momentum begins to build. Investors start to stampede. The stampede creates a mob mentality that seems to sweep everything along in its path until some unknowable top is reached, panic sets in, and everyone starts running for the door. Between 2000 and 2002, the Nasdaq index declined over 70 percent.

"Much has been written about panics and manias, much more than with the most outstretched intellect we are able to follow or conceive," wrote Walter Bagehot, first editor of the *Economist*. "But one thing is certain, that

Booms and Busts

	% Rise Bull Phase	Length of Bull Phase (months)	% Decline Peak to Trough	Length of Bear Phase (months)
Tulips (1634–1637) Netherlands	+5900%	36	−93%	10
Mississippi Shares France (1719–1721)	+6200%	13	−99%	13
South Sea Shares England (1719–1721)	+1000%	18	−84%	6
American Stocks U.S. (1923–1932)	+345%	71	−87%	33
Mexican Stocks Mexico (1978–1981)	+785%	30	−73%	18
Silver U.S. (1979–1982)	+710%	12	−88%	24
Gulf Stocks Kuwait (1978–1986)	+7000%	36	−98%	30
Hong Kong Stocks Hong Kong (1970–1974)	+1200%	28	−92%	20
Taiwan Stocks Taiwain (1986–1990)	+1168%	40	−80%	12

When the Japanese economy was roaring along, analysts praised the nation's government, corporate, and financial leaders for their close coordination and common purpose. By the 1990s, when the Japanese "miracle" was no more, commentators were pillorying the same people for their sluggish conformity and inability to think outside the box.

at particular times a great deal of stupid people have a great deal of stupid money. . . . At intervals, from causes which are not to the present purpose, the money of these people—the blind capital, as we call it, of the country—is particularly large and craving; it seeks for someone to devour it, and there is a 'plethora'; it finds someone, and there is 'speculation'; it is devoured, and there is 'panic.' "

As we see in the chart on the preceding page, adapted from Morgan Stanley Research, it doesn't matter what language the blind capital speaks. Stupid money is stupid money in any tongue.

Keeping Your Head When All About You Are Losing Theirs

How do you keep from getting caught up in the stampede when the market is either a raging bull or a roaring bear? It's not easy. No one wants to be left behind, no matter which direction the herd is moving. But more than four decades of tending to my own money and that of others has left me with a few principles that have served me well, no matter what direction stocks are headed. Here are 14 of the rules I try to follow.

- Remember that stock markets are always shifting between greed and fear. At the extreme of greed, great buys simply disappear, no matter how hard we might try to wish them into reality. At the extreme of fear, when all the excess has been wrung out of the market, great buys are all over the place.

- Remember, too, that the stock market always comes back, no matter how shocking the events that drive it down. Fear subsides; intrinsic value wins out. Within three years of John Kennedy's assassination, the S&P 500 was up nearly 21 percent. Within three years of the 1993 World Trade Center bombing, it was up almost 57 percent. Within three years of the December 7, 1941, attack on Pearl Harbor, the S&P 500 was up more than 81 percent.

- Define the sandbox you want to play in. I maintain a running list of 20 to 25 companies with records of consistent sales and earnings performance, with management committed to a defined strategy, and with strong franchises that are highly focused. I buy stock in those growth-value companies only when they are selling at sensible multiples, and I don't add new companies to the list unless I sell the weakest of those I own.

- Have a buy strategy and stick with that. I never take a huge stand at a single price because I've been humbled by the market too many times. Instead, if I think the price is within the range for a company I want to own, I begin to scale in: 25 percent of the desired holding today, 25 percent when market volatility drives the price down again, and so on. Putting orders in in advance can help prevent cold feet when the market turns really ugly. Yes, I'll miss the absolute bottom in all likelihood, but only the blindly lucky hit the bottom in any event.

- Stick with what you know. I stay highly focused: leading discount and home-improvement retailers, consumer staples, pharmaceuticals, package delivery, soft drinks, brewers, and financial service companies, all of whom are number-one in their field. Those are the companies I invest in because those are the products and services I can field test day in and day out through my own experience.

- Stick with who you are. Everyone has a different stomach. Whether you're buying stocks for yourself or for a client, realize that "too risky" and "too cautious" are completely subjective evaluations. When personality and portfolio get out of whack, bad decisions follow as day follows dawn.

- And stick with companies who know what they are, too. I invest only in companies that stay focused on their core competency and have a strong franchise. I avoid technology companies because industry changes are so rapid that most of them turn into commodity businesses with no lasting franchise.

- Always do due diligence. This is your money, your future security, and the security of your family. Invest it wisely, and only after thorough study. It's the mistakes that kill your investment performance. Evaluate the downside risk as much as the reward side, and you'll never have to be brilliant.

- Never make a buy or a sell decision in your broker's office or on the trading room floor. They're too close to the roar of the crowd. I always wait until I'm alone—shaving, maybe, or in the shower— to make up my mind. I'm safe there from the feeding frenzy that drew investors to companies like Enron, EMC, Global Crossing, Adelphia, Tyco, World Com, and too many others.

- Buy for the long term. If you were to die tomorrow, would this be a stock you would want your heirs to hold? It sounds morbid, but it's not a bad test to apply. Stocks should be for the ages, even if we won't survive them.

- Accept a little boredom in your life. Greedy management bent on making overpriced acquisitions gets the headlines, but good companies with superior management teams and a culture of teamwork, turning out good, usable, affordable products make money. Look for companies where there is a certainty of earnings predictability, ones selling at a reasonable multiple, generally no more than 50 or 60 percent greater than the rate of growth in earnings. I want the companies that best serve customer needs and desires whatever the product or service they are selling. If a company commands a growing share of its market at the revenue line, it would have to be incompetent not to increase its earnings meaningfully and consistently. Those are the dull measures of success that will set you apart from the stampeding crowd.

- Keep this in mind, too: The faster a stock has run up in value, the faster it is likely to run down. Almost no company can safely grow earnings faster than 15 to 20 percent a year without attracting fierce competition.
- It's the small things, not the big ones, that count. In baseball, home-run hitters get all the attention. Investing is simpler: Hit for average, swing for singles not the fences. This race is ultimately to the sure, not the swift; the tortoises, not the hares. Avoid losses. Have a truly long-term strategy and follow it consistently, and you'll finish in front.
- Never forget the miracle of compounding. My goal is to produce at least a 15 percent compound annual rate of return on average over a five-year period. Do that for 30 years, and your money will grow 66 fold. That's fast enough!

∼

The mass never comes up to the standard of its best member, but on the contrary degrades itself to a level with the lowest.

　　　　　　　　　　　　　　—Henry David Thoreau

2

RUMORS & SUGGESTIONS

Introduction

Bill Safire, who wrote the Foreword to this book, and I go back a long way, to high school and beyond. Bill grew up a city kid in New York, so he's not easily fooled. A lifetime in politics and, later, writing about politics and politicians has further honed his instinct to look dubiously on half-baked propositions. But even the wisest among us fall victim occasionally to the madness of crowds.

I remember so well sitting with Bill one evening over a drink a number of decades back as he told me about the can't-miss uranium stock he was planning to buy.

"Uranium?" I said to him, unable to hide my surprise. "Why on earth would you buy a uranium stock when there are so many good companies out there with known track records and solid earning streams? Even when the uranium companies aren't fly-by-night—and there are plenty of those—their earnings, if they have any, aren't predictable."

Well, it turns out Bill had plenty of reasons. A guy he had met at a party had suggested one of the uranium stocks just about the same time Bill picked up a rumor circulating through the political crowd in Washington that the government was about to throw its weight behind increased uranium use and production. It just stood to figure, he said. Opportunity was staring him in the face, and the timing was right, too.

I argued with him as hard as I could, but Bill wasn't about to be deterred. Everyone in his circle was talking about uranium, and all the talk was of the upside: soaring usage and huge potential profits, not the fact that no one yet had figured out how to make a real dime from any nuclear-related industry. Finally, I threw in the towel.

"It's your money," I told him.

Then it happened. As Bill went to light a cigarette—this was back when smoking was still socially acceptable—the entire match pack flared up in his hand.

"The Burning Bush!" he said to me with wonder in his eyes as we watched the pack turn to cinders in the ashtray. "God's voice. What's He trying to tell me?"

"Not to buy that damn uranium stock," I answered. And Bill didn't. Sometimes that's what it takes when rumor and suggestion work their wicked charms: divine intervention.

It shouldn't be so hard to resist such tiny items. A rumor is just a whisper in the dark. A suggestion doesn't have the force of a mandate behind it. We shrug such things off all the time. But a rumor is like a snowball: It starts small, but it can pick up mass and momentum as it rolls down the hill until what began in a hushed tone ends with the roar of an avalanche.

The name of the person who first claimed to have played the Beatles' song "Revolution 9" backwards and thus discovered, hidden in the vinyl grooves, the cryptic message "Turn me on, dead man" is lost to history. Nor do we know who first divined the words "I buried Paul" in the closing beats of "Strawberry Fields Forever." But out of such isolated whimsies grew a youth-culture obsession so powerful that when the first Beatle really did die in 1980—John Lennon, murdered by a crazed fan in Manhattan—it seemed almost the fulfillment of prophecy.

Even retroactively applied, truth and the semblance of believability give rumors legs. Like any noxious weed, rumors take hold and root where conditions are most propitious for growth. Another popular singer, Michael Jackson, is such a complexity of eccentricities, oddities, and outright weirdness that he's a rumor greenhouse all of his own, whether the subject is skin bleaching, facial reconstruction, or a case of infantilism.

The harder the rumor avalanche hits, too, the harder the core rumor can be to dislodge, even when contrary facts are made clear. The "second gunman" theory of John F. Kennedy's assassination lives on decades after the Warren Commission and other blue-ribbon investigators should have put it to bed, perhaps because we don't want to believe that a lone gunman could have laid waste to so many hopes and dreams. Many African Americans continue to believe in a secret "plan" by which white America holds them in subjugation because at least one of the elements of the alleged plan—spreading drug addiction through crack cocaine—has in fact wreaked such havoc in black neighborhoods.

The Federal Communications Commission has been struggling since 1974 to squelch a rumor that the late atheist activist Madalyn Murray O'Hair had circulated a petition meant to halt all religious references on radio and television. Not even O'Hair's death in 1995 could put a stop to the rumor mill. Six years later, the commission was still receiving comments and queries from alarmed citizens, via regular mail and e-mail, at the rate of about a hundred a month.

In the Internet, too, the rumor mill has found its perfect medium: a place where messages can be sent anonymously and multiply exponentially, and where little distinction is made between news, scandal, and raw guesswork. Add in the natural tendency to embellish a good tale as we pass it along, and an equal tendency to believe the extremes in what we hear, and it's easy to see how small misassumptions and slanders can become massive malignancies almost at the speed of light. Through the Internet, true believers also can set up cyber-communities where—like the Japanese soldiers dug into the mountains of Iwo Jima—they can hold out for months, even years, long after the war is over and everyone else has gone home.

Unlike rumors, which depend on a story line however flimsily constructed, suggestion relies on nothing more than the susceptibility of the listener. We've all been in the kitchen when someone questions whether the milk has turned sour or not. No matter how fresh the milk might actually be, it's almost impossible not to see it curdling before our eyes—and taste it going sour on our tongue—after the tiny seed of doubt has been sown.

A yawn is a suggestion, too, and an almost irresistible one, even when we're wide awake. Like the most powerful suggestions, yawns are contagious. Start one on a crowded subway, and you can watch it passing through the car and even, through the windows, from car to car, and from the passengers inside the train to those waiting on the platform for a different line to come along.

A friend tells of attending YMCA camp in 1954, the summer of the last great polio scare, when word suddenly began to spread from bunk to bunk during an afternoon rest period that the dreaded crippling disease could be caused by eating watermelon too close to the rind. Even for children not yet in their teens, the epidemiology made no sense, but watermelon had been served at lunch that day, and hungry as ever, many of the boys had dug almost into the rind for the last juicy morsels. Sure enough, before supper there was barely a camper who wasn't feeling achingly stiff in the limbs and envisioning himself spending the rest of his life in an iron lung.

That's the way it often is with the power of suggestion: It multiplies and spreads until dozens, sometimes hundreds and even thousands and millions of people seem to decide simultaneously on the epic importance of something with little intrinsic value or the complete validity of something with little underlying truth. Fads are nothing more than the rapid growth of such mass contagion whether the object of the frenzy is the newest must-have gift—Hula Hoops, Cabbage Patch Kids, Beanie Babies, collapsible scooters—or the newest must-see entertainer, from Frank Sinatra to Britney Spears.

Not all crazes end benignly, at Toys "R" Us or in the mosh pit. So powerful can be the pull of a craze that it begins to blur the line between imagination and reality, between what's possible in a fantasy world and what's possible and allowable in an actual one. Superman comic books and the 1950s TV show starring George Reeves convinced more than one six year old to tie a towel around his neck and try flying from the garage roof, sometimes with disastrous results. The wildly popular—and often extremely violent—"Gothic" Internet games have been implicated in numerous cases of murder and mayhem by participants who couldn't separate cyberreality from the everyday variety.

Inevitably, crazes heighten emotion, and in a heightened emotional state, behavior is always unpredictable. More than two centuries ago, Johann Wolfgang von Goethe's coming-of-age novel, *The Sorrows of Young Werther,* so closely identified unrequited youthful love with suicidal longing that a number of romantically frustrated German youths took their lives while clutching copies of Goethe's great work. (Goethe himself seems to have used writing the book as a sort of therapy to get over the worst of his own miseries.)

Happily, the power of rumor and suggestion, and the herd instinct they play upon, can be harnessed toward positive ends as well. One study found that college students tended to binge drink because they consistently overestimated the amount of alcohol their fellow students consumed. To reverse the trend, Northern Illinois University in 1990 launched an ad campaign to inform students that, contrary to rumor, most students had fewer than five drinks when they partied. By the end of the decade, the *New York Times Magazine* reported, heavy drinking on the campus was down by more than 40 percent.

Sometimes, too, the intersection of rumor and suggestion can be so strong that it creates its own reality, as it did in this exchange—recorded by the Puritan preacher Cotton Mather and worthy of a Stalin-era courtroom—during the famous Salem witch trials of 1692. At trial is Mary Lacey, accused of practicing witchcraft.

MAGISTRATE: Do you acknowledge now you are a witch?

MARY LACEY: Yes.

MAGISTRATE: How long have you been a witch?

LACEY: Not above a week.

MAGISTRATE: Did the Devil appear to you?

LACEY: Yes.

MAGISTRATE: In what shape?

LACEY: In the shape of a horse.

MAGISTRATE: What did he say to you?

LACEY: He bid me not to be afraid of any thing, and he would bring me out; but he has proved a liar from the beginning.

A "witch" hanging in Scotland, 1678. Beginning about 1450 and extending some 250 years, at least 10,000 women were charged with witchcraft in Europe, and many of them were subjected to such torture in the search for "confessions" that death by hanging must have seemed almost a blessing. (The Granger Collection, New York)

MAGISTRATE: Did he bid you worship him?

LACEY: Yes; he bid me also to afflict persons.

MAGISTRATE: Who did the Devil bid you afflict?

LACEY: Timothy Swan. Richard Carrier comes often a-nights and has me to afflict persons.

MAGISTRATE: Did you at any time ride upon a stick or pole?

LACEY: Yes.

MAGISTRATE: How high?

LACEY: Sometimes above the trees.

Twenty witches were executed in Salem before the trials were halted by the governor of Massachusetts colony, but not Mary Lacey. For accepting the suggestions of her inquisitor and seeing the world as he would have her see it, Lacey's life was spared.

Chicken Licken's
Apocalypse Now

Even more so than the rest of the world, the business world seems to propel itself along by embracing extremes: If the market isn't about to explode, it's on the verge of a nosedive. Either the bull is roaring or the bear is out. Fueled by dreams of great profit, or fear of great loss, suggestions turn into rumors with lightning speed, and rumors into "facts" just as quickly, backed up by sophisticated charts and analyses.

Sometimes it takes a good children's story to show us just how easily the mob can get carried away, whether the subject is plunging stock prices or a falling sky. Indeed, in this traditional version of the "Chicken Little" fable—taken from the Classic Volland Edition of *Great Children's Stories* (Harvard University Press)—we can see nearly all the elements of crowd psychology at work that Edward Alsworth Ross describes in his seminal 1919 text, *Social Psychology*.

"To the degree that feeling is intensified," Ross writes, "reason is paralyzed. In general, strong emotion inhibits the intellectual processes. In a sudden crisis we expect the sane act from the man who is 'cool,' who has not 'lost his head.' Now, the very hurly-burly of the crowd tends to distraction. Then, the high pitch of feeling to which the crowd gradually works up checks thinking and results in a temporary imbecility. There is no question that, taken herdwise, people are less sane and sensible than they are dispersed. . . .

"Under these conditions—heightened suggestibility and emotion, arrested thinking—three things will happen when an impulse, whether emanating from a spectacle, an event, or a leader, runs through the crowd.

1. *Extension.* By sheer contagion it extends to unsympathetic persons. . . .
2. *Intensification.* Each individual impressed feels more intensely the moment he perceives that so many others share his feeling. Hence, a secondary wave, a reverberation, runs through the crowd that is becoming aware of itself.
3. *Predisposition.* The perceived unison begets a sympathy that makes like response easier the next time."

One more thing the antics of Chicken Licken, Henny Penny, Goosey Loosey, and the rest teach us about the behavior of crowds: When the sky is falling, you can run but you can't hide, at least not with Foxy Woxy.

One day when Chicken Licken was scratching among the leaves, an acorn fell out of a tree and struck her on the tail. "Oh," said Chicken Licken, "the sky is falling! I am going to tell the King."

So she went along and went along until she met Henny Penny.

"Good morning, Chicken Licken, where are you going?" said Henny Penny.

"Oh, Henny Penny, the sky is falling and I am going to tell the King!"

"How do you know the sky is falling?" asked Henny Penny.

"I saw it with my own eyes, I heard it with my own ears, and a piece of it fell on my tail!" said Chicken Licken. "Then I will go with you," said Henny Penny.

So they went along and went along until they met Cocky Locky.

"Good morning, Henny Penny and Chicken Licken," said Cocky Locky, "where are you going?" "Oh, Cocky Locky, the sky is falling, and we are going to tell the King!"

"How do you know the sky is falling?" asked Cocky Locky.

"Chicken Licken told me," said Henny Penny.

"I saw it with my own eyes, I heard it with my own ears, and a piece of it fell on my tail!" said Chicken Licken.

"Then I will go with you," said Cocky Locky, "and we will tell the King."

So they went along and went along until they met Ducky Daddles.

"Good morning, Cocky Locky, Henny Penny, and Chicken Licken," said Ducky Daddles, "where are you going?"

"Oh, Ducky Daddles, the sky is falling and we are going to tell the King!"

"How do you know the sky is falling?" asked Ducky Daddles.

"Henny Penny told me," said Cocky Locky.

"Chicken Licken told me," said Henny Penny.

"I saw it with my own eyes, I heard it with my own ears, and a piece of it fell on my tail!" said Chicken Licken.

"Then I will go with you," said Ducky Daddles, "and we will tell the King."

So they went along and went along until they met Goosey Loosey.

"Good morning, Ducky Daddles, Cocky Locky, Henny Penny, and Chicken Licken," said Goosey Loosey, "where are you going?"

"Oh, Goosey Loosey, the sky is falling and we are going to tell the King!"

"How do you know the sky is falling?" asked Goosey Loosey.

"Cocky Locky told me," said Ducky Daddles.

"Henny Penny told me," said Cocky Locky.

"Chicken Licken told me," said Henny Penny.

"I saw it with my own eyes, I heard it with my own ears, and a piece of it fell on my tail!" said Chicken Licken.

"Then I will go with you," said Goosey Loosey, "and we will tell the King!"

So they went along and went along until they met Turkey Lurkey.

George Bellows, *The Crowd* (1923)

"Good morning, Goosey Loosey, Ducky Daddles, Cocky Locky, Henny Penny, and Chicken Licken," said Turkey Lurkey, "where are you going?"

"Oh, Turkey Lurkey, the sky is falling and we are going to tell the King!"

"How do you know the sky is falling?" asked Turkey Lurkey.

"Ducky Daddles told me," said Goosey Loosey.

"Cocky Locky told me," said Ducky Daddles.

"Henny Penny told me," said Cocky Locky.

"Chicken Licken told me," said Henny Penny.

"I saw it with my own eyes, I heard it with my own ears, and a piece of it fell on my tail!" said Chicken Licken.

"Then I will go with you," said Turkey Lurkey, "and we will tell the King!"

So they went along and went along until they met Foxy Woxy.

"Good morning, Turkey Lurkey, Goosey Loosey, Ducky Daddles, Cocky Locky, Henny Penny, and Chicken Licken," said Foxy Woxy, "where are you going?"

"Oh, Foxy Woxy, the sky is falling and we are going to tell the King!"

"How do you know the sky is falling?" asked Foxy Woxy.

"Goosey Loosey told me," said Turkey Lurkey.

"Ducky Daddles told me," said Goosey Loosey.

"Cocky Locky told me," said Ducky Daddles.

"Henny Penny told me," said Cocky Locky.

"Chicken Licken told me," said Henny Penny.

"I saw it with my own eyes, I heard it with my own ears, and a piece of it fell on my tail," said Chicken Licken.

"Then we will run, we will run to my den," said Foxy Woxy, "and I will tell the King."

So they all ran to Foxy Woxy's den, and the King was never told that the sky was falling.

~

Rumor is a pipe
Blown by surmises, jealousies, conjectures . . .
—William Shakespeare, *King Henry IV*

Something from Nothing:
The Alchemy of Suggestion

Anyone who has lived through the wild market swings brought on by the frequently cryptic comments of Federal Reserve Chairman Alan Greenspan doesn't need to be told about the power of rumor and suggestion to affect events in the real world, not just in children's stories. The short-term fortunes of powerful global corporations get held ransom by hints of lawsuits and hunches that a government agency might see fit to launch an investigation. Base your financial decisions on these "sky is falling" scenarios and you'll end up as exhausted and trapped as Chicken Licken, and no richer.

One of the earliest recorded incidents of a suggestion that quickly grew to frightening dimensions took place in the year 1212, in what became known as the Children's Crusade led by a peasant boy named Stephen from near the French town of Vendome and Nicholas, a German boy from Cologne. A chronicler of the time describes the scene:

> In this year occurred an outstanding thing and one much to be marveled at, for it is unheard of throughout the ages. About the time of Easter and Pentecost, without anyone having preached or called for it and prompted by I know not what spirit, many thousands of boys, ranging in age from six years to full maturity, left the plows or carts which they were driving, the flocks which they were pasturing, and anything else which they were doing. This they did despite the wishes of their parents, relatives, and friends who sought to make them draw back. Suddenly one ran after another to take the cross. Thus, by groups of twenty, or fifty, or a hundred, they put up banners and began to journey to Jerusalem.

Although their numbers eventually swelled to some 50,000, the children never reached their goal. At Marseilles and other ports from which they had hoped to sail to the Holy Land, many of the girls were forced into brothels and the boys sold to Egyptian slavers. "One thing is sure," the chronicler notes: "that of the many thousands who rose up, only very few returned."

The children of Bay Harbor Elementary School in Miami Beach had nothing so grand as a crusade in mind when they showed up for classes one school day in May 1974. But as Berton Roueché recounts in this excerpt from the August 21, 1978, issue of the *New Yorker*, the day was to unfold as no one could have foreseen, and the power of suggestion to impel group behavior would be at the crux of events.

Dr. Joel L. Nitzkin, chief of the Office of Consumer Protection, a section of the Dade County, Florida, Department of Public Health, sat crouched (he is six feet nine) at his desk in the Civic Center complex in downtown Miami, stirring a mug of coffee that his secretary had just brought in. It was around half past ten on a sunny Monday morning in May—May 13, 1974. His telephone rang. He put down his coffee and picked up the phone and heard the voice of a colleague, Martha Sonderegger, the department's assistant nursing director. Miss Sonderegger was calling to report that her Miami Beach unit had just received a call for help—for the services of a team of public-health nurses—from the Bay Harbor Elementary School. There had been a pipe break or a leak of some kind, Miss Sonderegger had been told, and the school was engulfed in a pall of poison gas. Many of the children were ill, and some had been taken to a neighborhood hospital by the rescue squad of the municipal fire department. Dr. Nitzkin listened, considered.

He said, "What do you think, Martha?"

"It sounds a little strange."

"I think so, too."

"But I'm sending a team of nurses."

"Yes," Dr. Nitzkin said. "Of course. And I think I'd better drive out to the school and take a look myself."

He thanked her and hung up—and then picked up the phone again. He made two quick calls. One was to an industrial hygienist named Carl DiSalvo, in the Division of Environmental Health. The other was to a staff physician, named Myriam Enriquez, in the Disease Control Section. He asked Dr. Enriquez to meet him at once at his car; as for Mr. DiSalvo, he was already on his way to the school. Dr. Nitzkin untangled his legs and got up. He was out of his office in two easy, five-foot strides. His coffee cooled on his desk, untasted and forgotten.

Dr. Nitzkin is no longer associated with the Dade County Department of Public Health. He has moved up, both professionally and geographically, to Rochester, New York, where he now serves as director of the Monroe County Department of Health, and it was there, on a winter day, that I talked with him about the summons to the Bay Harbor Elementary School. His recollection was undimmed, indelible.

"I remember it was hot," he told me, standing at his office window and gazing out through the palm trees in his memory at the bare maples and last night's foot of new snow. "Warm, anyway—warm enough to make me think that the 'poison gas' at the school might have something to do with the air-conditioning system. And I remember my first sight of the school. The scene was complete pandemonium. It had the look of a disaster. We had to park half a block away, because the school parking lot was full of trucks and vans and cars of all kinds—all parked every which way. Ambulances. Fire equipment. Police cars. All with their flashers flashing. And the media—they were swarming. Newspaper reporters and photographers. Radio people with microphones. Television cameras from four local stations. And even—good God!—local dignitaries. Members of the Dade County School Board. Members of the Bay Harbor Town Council. And neighbors and passersby and parents all rushing around. I had never seen anything like it, and I had to wonder how come. But the explanation, it turned out, was simple enough. The school had called the fire department, and the fire department had called the rescue squad—and the media all monitor the fire department's radio frequency. There was one oasis of calm and order. That was the children. They had been marched out of the building in fire-drill formation and were lined up quietly in the shade of some trees at the far end of the school grounds. There were a lot of them—several hundred, it looked like. Which was reassuring. I had got the impression that most of the school had been stricken by whatever the trouble was. Dr. Enriquez and I cut through the mob, looking for someone in charge. It turned out that the school principal was away somewhere at a meeting. We asked around and were finally directed to the head secretary. She was the person nominally in charge, but you couldn't say she was in control. Nobody was in control.

"She and Dr. Enriquez and I talked for a moment at the entrance to the building. The building was standard design for contemporary Florida schools. The entrance hall ran back to a cross corridor that led to the class-rooms. The other school facilities were off the entrance hall. The offices, the clinic, and the library were on the right-hand side. On the left were the teachers' lounge, the cafetorium, and the kitchen. A cafetorium is a room that doubles as an auditorium and a cafeteria. The secretary gave us all the information she had. It was her understanding that there had been a gas leak of some kind. That was what she had heard. But she had seen the first victim with her own eyes. The first victim was an eleven-year-old girl in the fifth grade. I'll call her Sandy. Sandy was a member of a chorus of around a hundred and seventy-five fourth, fifth, and sixth graders who had assembled with the music teacher in the cafetorium at nine o'clock to rehearse for a schoolwide musical program. Halfway through the hour—this, I should say, was constructed later—she began to feel sick. She slipped out of the cafetorium. She was seen by some of the students but not by the teacher. She went across the hall to the clinic and went and collapsed on a couch. The clinic staff was off duty at the moment, but the secretary happened to catch sight of her, and went in and found her lying there unconscious. She tried to revive her—with smelling salts!"

"My mother used to carry smelling salts," I said.

"Yes. It was rather sweet, I thought. Well, anyway, Sandy didn't respond, and that very naturally alarmed the secretary. And so she very naturally called for help. She called the fire department. Sandy was still unconscious when the fire-rescue squad arrived, and they didn't waste any time. They put her on a stretcher and took her off to the hospital—North Shore Hospital. Then another child got sick, and another, and another. That's when our nursing unit was called. Seven children were sick enough to also be rushed to the hospital after Sandy went. Around twenty-five others were sick enough to be sent home. The school called their parents, and they came and picked them up. Another forty or so were being treated here at the school. They were in the cafetorium." Dr. Nitzkin raised his eyebrows. "That's what the secretary said—in the cafetorium! Myriam Enriquez and I exchanged a look. Wasn't the cafetorium where Sandy became ill, I asked. Where the poison gas must have first appeared? The secretary looked baffled. She said she didn't know anything about that. She had first seen Sandy in the clinic. All she knew was that the sick children still at the school were being treated in the cafetorium.

"We left the secretary and went on into the school. I think we were both in the same uncomfortable state of mind.

"The situation still felt the way it had to Martha Sonderegger. It felt strange. There was also a strange smell in the place. We smelled it the minute we stepped into the hall. It wasn't unpleasant—just strong. We couldn't place it. Well, that was what Carl DiSalvo was here for. He would work it out. I hadn't seen him, but I knew he was somewhere in the building. We went on to the cafetorium. There was the sound of many voices. It sounded like a mammoth cocktail party. We went into a big room full of people, full of uniforms. Nurses. Police. Fire-rescue workers, in their white coveralls. And a lot of other people. The sick children were stretched out here and there. I could still smell the strange smell, but it was fainter—much fainter—here. Dr. Enriquez and I separated. She had her clinical tests to make. I was the epidemiologist. I walked around the room and looked, and talked to some of the children. The clinical picture was rather curious. There was an unusual variety of signs and symptoms. Headache. Dizziness. Chills. Abdominal pain. Shortness of breath. Weakness. I noticed two kids who were obviously hyperventilating, breathing very fast and deep. That was an interesting symptom.

"I stood and thought for a moment. I began to get a glimmer of a glimmer. I went across the hall to an office and found a telephone and called the emergency room at North Shore Hospital and talked to the doctor on duty there. He knew about the children from the Bay Harbor school. He said they were in satisfactory condition. He said they seemed to be feeling better. He said he didn't have results on all of the lab tests yet, but the findings he had seen seemed to be essentially normal. My glimmer still glimmered. I started back to the cafetorium, and ran into DiSalvo. He had been looking for me. He had made a quick inspection of the physical environment of the building and he hadn't turned up any tangible factors—any gases or fumes or allergens—that could have caused any kind of illness. I mentioned the funny smell. He laughed. He had checked it out. It came from an adhesive used to secure a new carpet in the library. The adhesive was in no way toxic. Anyway, the carpet had been laid a good two weeks earlier. DiSalvo was satisfied with his preliminary findings, but he was going to settle down and do the usual full-scale comprehensive survey. I was satisfied, too. I was more than willing to drop the idea of a toxic gas. I had never really believed it. And I was also satisfied that we could rule out a bacterial or viral cause of the trouble. The incubation period—the interval between exposure and the onset of illness—was much too short. And the symptoms were also wrong.

"I left DiSalvo and went back to the cafetorium, and I remember looking at my watch. It was eleven-thirty. I had been at the school a scant twenty minutes. It felt like forever. But then, all of a sudden, things began to move. I entered the cafetorium this time by a side door at the kitchen end of the room, and there was a woman standing there—one of the kitchen staff. The dietitian, maybe. An authoritative woman, anyway. She called me over. And—Was it some look in my eye? I don't know. But she said, 'Aren't you a doctor?' I said I was. 'Well,' she said, 'then why don't you do something? Why don't you straighten out this mess? This is all perfectly ridiculous. You know as well as I do that there's nothing the matter with these kids. Get them up on their feet! Get them out of here! They're in the way! I have to start setting up for lunch.'

"I must have stood and gaped at her. I'd had a funny feeling—a deep-down, gut suspicion—from the very beginning of the case that there was something not quite right about it. I'd got a glimmer when I saw those two kids hyperventilating. Hyperventilation is a classic psychosomatic anxiety reaction. And now the truth finally hit me. A memory rose up in my mind. I knew what I was seeing here. Something very like this had happened just a year before in an elementary school in a little town in Alabama—Berry, Alabama. The dietician was right. But she was also wrong. She was right about there being nothing fundamentally the matter with the kids. But she was wrong in thinking that all those aches and pains and nausea were illusory.

They were real, all right. And this was a real epidemic. It was an epidemic of mass hysteria."

Having decided upon a diagnosis of mass hysteria, Roueché writes, Dr. Nitzkin then took what might have been the hardest action of all. With the media hanging on to his every word, Nitzkin told worried parents and teachers that the only way to bring the outbreak under control was for the school to get back to normal. Clear the cafetorium so the kitchen staff could get set up for lunch, he said. Get the children back into their classrooms. Amazingly (but not so amazingly really), the course of treatment worked.

Eventually, as part of his effort to understand the outbreak, Dr. Nitzkin and his team built a clinical study around a student questionnaire that focused on the 73 students, out of an enrollment of 450, who had reported at least some symptoms. We pick the story up there:

"The questionnaire provided some very interesting information. The comments of some of the children who reported feeling sick that morning were particularly revealing. These were mostly in response to the question 'When you got sick, did you know that other children were sick, too?' I'll read you some of the comments. One girl answered, 'Yes, because Sandy fainted.' Another wrote, 'Yes—a lot of kids. I started to feel sick between Music and Language Arts, and then they carried me outside.' Another girl answered, 'I just knew that a boy vomited.' Her only symptom was nausea. Another girl wrote, 'Yes—Sandy was sick.' And a boy—one of the few boys— wrote, 'Yes, and after Sandy got sick and there was a fire drill, and when everybody was walking out of the building, I felt like a small headache.' Well, you get the drift. We also talked to Sandy. She turned out to be pretty much as expected. I mean, she was the right type. She was attractive. She was a good student. She was precocious. And she was very popular. She was looked up to."

"She was a kind of leader?" I asked. "She set the pattern?"

"Yes," he said. "I think you could say that."

"But what about her?" I asked. "What made her get sick?"

Dr. Nitzkin looked at me. "Oh," he said. "Sandy was really sick. She had some sort of virus. All that standing and singing in place was too much for her. She just passed out."

Frank Sinatra was already on his way to stardom when he broke from the Tommy Dorsey Band in 1942. Two years later, when he put on a series of performances at New York City's Paramount Theater, 10,000 fans jammed the ticket window and twice as many more spilled into Times Square. Inside the theater, as shown here, Sinatra left the girls swooning, and parents and social commentators once again were mystified by his enormous popularity. (AP/Wide World Photo)

In 1956, a dozen years after Frank Sinatra had taken New York by storm, Elvis Presley did the same, gyrating his way through "Hound Dog" and "Don't Be Cruel" on TV's popular *The Ed Sullivan Show*. That summer Elvis returned to his hometown of Tupelo, Mississippi, to play before this crowd of thousands at the Mississippi-Alabama State Fair. "The King" had been crowned. (© Bettmann/CORBIS)

Beatlemania swept both sides of the Atlantic. In New York City, fans rushed the fire escapes of the elegant Plaza Hotel after the Beatles checked in during their first trip to America. Here, London fans test the legendary reserve of their bobbies as they try to storm Buckingham Palace during a visit by the suddenly famous Fab Four. (© Hulton-Deutsch Collections/CORBIS)

Tom Wolfe on
the Beatles

Mass hysteria can create mass wants and needs as easily as it creates mass sickness. When individual wills run together, the desire of a few leaders—the "Sandys" of the pack—quickly become the desire of all the pack. We see this in politics all the time, and in business as well. So great was the hysteria generated by the rapid run up in high-tech stocks during the dot-com boom that even seasoned venture capitalists were tripping over each other to give money to wet-behind-the-ears entrepreneurs who had nothing more than a brightly colored business plan to offer for sale.

As marketers so well know, the pull of mass hysteria can be especially strong for teenagers. Anxious to be accepted by their peers and uncertain where they fit in the world, teens rush to new products like ants to a picnic lunch. Nowhere is this more evident than with popular music. Songs, albums, individual performers, and groups sweep across the teen-culture landscape like wildfire. In arenas and stadiums where the most famous acts play, 16 year olds who couldn't agree with their parents about the time of day suddenly act as if they were all connected to a single heart, a single mind.

Mass music purveyors like MTV have certainly accelerated the trend toward a collective audience agreement over who's hot and who's not, but mass hysteria over musical performers was going on long before cable TV. Frank Sinatra had his bobby-soxers in the 1940s. Elvis Presley scandalized parents and thrilled their children with the first glimmer of the sexual revolution in the 1950s. Then in the 1960s came the biggest act of all—so hot that one of its members once described the group, only half in jest, as "more popular than Jesus Christ."

Novelist and social critic Tom Wolfe was a reporter for the now-defunct *New York Herald Tribune* when the Beatles first set foot in the United States. He filed this dispatch on B-Day: February 7, 1964.

By 6:30 a.m., half the kids from South Orange, N.J., to Seaford, [Long Island], were already up with their transistors plugged in their skulls. It was like a civil defense network or something. You could turn anywhere on the dial, WMCA, WCBS, WINS, almost any place, and get the bulletins: "It's B-Day! 6:30 a.m.! The Beatles left London

"Whoever he is, he's got charisma."

30 minutes ago! They're 30 minutes out over the Atlantic Ocean! Heading for New York!"

By 1 p.m. about 4,000 kids had finessed school and come skipping and screaming into the international terminal at Kennedy Airport. It took 110 police to herd them. At 1:20 p.m., the Beatles' jet arrived from London.

The Beatles left the plane and headed for customs inspection and everybody got their first live look at the Beatles' hair style, which is a mop effect that covers the forehead, some of the ears and most of the back of the neck. To get a better look, the kids came plunging down the observation deck, and some of them already had their combs out, raking their hair down over their foreheads as they ran.

Then they were crowding around the plate-glass windows overlooking the customs section, stomping on the floor in unison, some of them beating time by bouncing off the windows.

The Beatles—George Harrison, 20; John Lennon, 23; Ringo Starr, 23; and Paul McCartney, 21—are all short, slight kids from Liverpool who wear four-button coats, stovepipe pants, ankle-high black boots with Cuban heels. And droll looks on their faces. Their name is a play on the word "beat."

They went into a small room for a press conference, while some of the girls tried to throw themselves over a retaining wall.

Somebody motioned to the screaming crowds outside. "Aren't you embarrassed by all this lunacy?"

"No," said John Lennon. "It's crazy."

"What do you think of Beethoven?"

"He's crazy," said Lennon. "Especially the poems. Lovely writer."

In the two years in which they have risen from a Liverpool rock-and-roll dive group to the hottest performers in the record business, they had seen much of this wildness before. What really got them were the American teenage car sorties.

The Beatles left the airport in four Cadillac limousines, one Beatle to a limousine, heading for the Plaza Hotel in Manhattan. The first sortie came almost immediately. Five kids in a powder blue Ford overtook the caravan on the expressway, and as they passed each Beatle, one guy hung out the back window and waved a red blanket.

A white convertible came up second, with the word BEETLES scratched on both sides in the dust. A police car was close behind that one with the siren going and the alarm light rolling, but the kids, a girl at the wheel and two guys in the back seat, waved at each Beatle before pulling over to the exit with the cops gesturing at them.

Manufactured for pennies and sold for $1.98 each, the Hula Hoop is one of the great examples of how consumer behavior builds upon itself. The girl next door gets a Hula Hoop, and your daughter has to have one. Your daughter gets one, and now two girls have them and four more have to get them, and only an official Hula Hoop will do no matter how similar a knockoff brand might be. Strangely, when a fad hits critical mass, it becomes very specific in its terms. These six hoops, photographed in action on a New York-area playground, were among the 100 million units Wham-O manufacturing sold worldwide in 1958, the year the hoop was introduced.

In the second limousine, Brian Sommerville, the Beatles' press agent, said to one of the Beatles, George Harrison: "Did you see that, George?"

Harrison looked at the convertible with its emblem in the dust and said "They misspelled Beatles."

But the third sortie succeeded all the way. A good-looking brunette, who said her name was Caroline Reynolds, of New Canaan, Conn., and Wellesley College, had paid a cab driver $10 to follow the caravan all the way into town. She cruised by each Beatle, smiling faintly, and finally caught up with George Harrison's limousine at a light at Third Avenue and 63rd St.

"How does one go about meeting a Beatle?" she said out of the window.

"One says hello," said Harrison out the window.

"Hello!" she said. "Eight more will be down from Wellesley." Then the light changed and the caravan was off again.

At the Plaza Hotel, there were police everywhere. The Plaza, on Central Park South just off Fifth Ave., is one of the most sedate hotels in New York. The Plaza was petrified. The Plaza accepted the Beatles' reservations months ago, before knowing it was a rock-and-roll group that attracts teenage riots.

About 500 teenagers, most of them girls, had shown up at the Plaza. The police had herded most of them behind barricades in the square between the hotel and the avenue. Every entrance to the hotel was guarded. The screams started as soon as the first limousine came into view.

The Beatles jumped out fast at the Fifth Avenue entrance. The teenagers had all been kept at bay. Old ladies ran up and touched the Beatles on their arms and backs as they ran up the stairs.

After they got to the Plaza the Beatles rested up for a round of television appearances (the Ed Sullivan Show, Sunday), recordings (Capitol Records), concerts (Carnegie Hall, Wednesday) and a tour (Washington, Miami). The kids were still hanging around the Plaza hours after they went inside. One group of girls asked everybody who came out, "Did you see the Beatles? Did you touch them?"

A policeman came up, and one of them yelled, "He touched a Beatle! I saw him!" The girls jumped on the cop's arms and back, but it wasn't a mob assault. There were goony smiles all over their faces.

～

In a world in which so many people wear the same clothes, live in the same house, eat the same dinner, and say the same things, blessed are the individuals who are not lost in the mob, who have their own thoughts, and live their own lives.

—Hamilton Wright Mabie

Waiting for Godot

Much of the strength of rumor and suggestion comes from the natural human tendency to migrate to the best or worst possibilities in whatever situation presents itself. Let the weatherperson announce that a few inches of snow might fall tomorrow, and supermarkets begin to fill up with anxious customers in search of enough basics to see them through a once-every-hundred-years blizzard. If a few inches, why not a few feet? If a few feet, why not yards of the white stuff?

Similarly, when a leading business analyst announces that this company or that might be in for a rough patch or a good one, the trajectory of its stock is likely to far outrun the trajectory of the company's earnings. "Rough times" translates to disastrous ones in investors' minds as readily as "good times" conjures up streets paved with gold. Either way, investors tend to act en masse, which only exaggerates the exaggeration. That's the price of our humanity: We have imaginations.

Snow melts, at least in the lower 48 states, and money is only money, although worry about it has been known to cause many a panic. When eternity appears to be at stake, the rush toward a crowd mentality and the extremes of possibility can be all the greater. The almost unbelievable mass suicide that took place at Jonestown in the South American jungle in 1978, when more than 900 followers of Jim Jones took their lives, can be attributed to many factors: a brainwashing so thorough that Jones's believers regularly rehearsed their communal death, the murder of a United States congressman who had come to Guyana to investigate Jones and his People's Temple, and Jones's own twisted mind. Wherever one places the blame, the simple fact is that, in the pursuit of eternity, hundreds upon hundreds of people had ceded their own individual reason to a singular group vision that impelled them toward bizarre actions. In that regard, Jonestown has a long lineage in American history.

In 1831, a New York lay preacher named William Miller announced that his reading of the Bible had revealed to him that the world would end with the final Judgment in the early 1840s. Miller would finally settle on October 22, 1844, by which time his followers—the forerunners of today's Adventist movement—had grown to nearly a million in number. While not nearly so gruesome as the Jonestown affair, the last days of Miller's vision were stunning nonetheless. This anonymous description is taken from a history of Philadelphia published in 1884.

The excitement in Philadelphia had been growing for two or more years, and by the summer of 1844 it was indescribable. The Millerite Church was on Julianna Street, between Wood and Callowhill, and there Miller's followers met night and day, and watched the stars and sun, and prayed and warned the unrepentant that the "Day of Judgment was at hand."

Many of them began to sell their houses at prices which were merely nominal. Others gave away their personal effects, shut up their business, or vacated their houses. On a store on Fifth Street, above Chestnut, was a placard which read thus:

"This shop is closed in honor of the King of Kings who will appear about the 20th of October. Get ready friends to crown Him Lord of all." . . . People laboring under the excitement went mad.

On one occasion all the windows of a meeting-house were surrounded at night by a crowd of young fellows, and at a given signal the darkness and gloom were made lurid by flaming torches, and the air resounded with the roar of firecrackers. The Saints inside went wild with terror, for they thought the fiery whirlwind was come.

The Sunday before the final day was an eventful one. The Julianna Street Chapel was crowded. A mob of unbelievers on the pavements stoned the windows and hooted at the worshippers. The police of Northern Liberties, and Spring Garden, and a sheriff's posse, headed by Morton McMichael, were on hand to quell the threatened disturbance. The members of the congregation repaired to their homes, and after, in many cases, leaving their doors and windows open, and giving away their furniture, set out for the suburban districts. A large number went over into New Jersey, but their chief party assembled in Isaac Yocomb's field on the Darby Road, three miles and a half from the Market Street bridge. While here a furious hurricane strengthened the faith of the Millerites and struck awful terror to the souls of the timid. It swept over the city, destroying shipping and demolishing houses . . .

The crowd at Darby was gathered in two tents, but so great was it that the children for two days were obliged to run about the fields,

exposed to the pelting of a pitiless storm, and crying for their parents. The parents, clad in their white ascension robes, were almost exhausted for want of food, slept on the cold wet ground, and prayed and hymned and groaned incessantly.

At midnight on the 22nd, the Bridegroom was to come, and a rain of fire was to descend from the heavens, and the Saints were to be gathered up in a whirlwind. There they stood on that black, tempestuous October night, shivering with cold and fear—their faces upturned, and every eye strained to catch a beam of the awful light piercing the clouds. The morning broke, and with it came the end of the delusion. The assemblage dispersed in despair, and slunk away silently and downcast to their houses.

~

You can talk a mob into anything.
                              —John Ruskin, *Sesame and Lilies*

Roswell, New Mexico: Things That Go Bump in the Night

A rumor prospers best where people are most predisposed to accept its underlying premises. The supposed wonders of biotechnology, for example, launched an investment and buying spree in biotech businesses and stocks because so many of us wanted to believe that in the marriage of biology and technology waited the answer to medical problems that have bedeviled humankind for millennia. When biotech failed to live up to its promise, the potential wonders of gene therapy took its place, for all of the same reasons, this time magnified by the sheer dazzling brilliance of the science involved. In the long run, gene therapy will almost certainly live up to its promise, and biotechnology, too. Meanwhile, a lot of money has been used as tinder for a fire that's barely sparking.

In Roswell, New Mexico, the rumors of downed flying saucers and captured alien life forms might have found the perfect match with a willing audience. A city of some 50,000 people set on the moonscapelike eastern plains of New Mexico, Roswell had been home in the 1920s to some of Robert Goddard's first pioneering tests in rocketry. Nearly two decades later, the flight crews that would carry the only atomic bombs ever dropped in warfare were stationed at the Roswell Army Airfield. The White Sands Missile Range is an hour or so away. So is the Trinity test site where the first A-bomb was exploded. Residents, in short, were used to keeping a wary eye on the heavens, and as Joseph Falco wrote in *Cyberwest* magazine, "If you were an alien on routine anthropological patrol, and you detected a civilization's first atomic blast, you would head to the Roswell area, too."

Predisposition, though, can only partially explain what Roswell has become. Home to not one but two museums—the Enigma UFO Museum and the grandly named International UFO Museum and Research Center—Roswell has been the subject of an astounding array of books, grade-B movies, bad TV shows, and nearly infinite Internet postings devoted to the alien spacecraft that supposedly crashed there and to the extraterrestrial life form that is said to be preserved still in a secret government lab. To transform its predisposition into what is both a national joke and a kind of holy shrine, Roswell needed a precipitating event, and that came in the form of a front-page article that appeared in the *Roswell Daily Record* on Tuesday, July 8, 1947.

Note in it the classic elements that help to turn rumor into reality: a veneer of detail, the imprimatur of authority, and what former *Washington Post* editor Ben Bradlee used to call a "holy shit" story, in this case unchallenged by sober minds.

RAAF Captures Flying Saucer on Ranch in Roswell Region

No Details of Flying Disk Are Revealed.
Roswell Hardware Man and Wife Report Disk Seen.

The intelligence office of the 509th Bombardment Group at Roswell Army Airfield announced at noon today that the field has come into possession of a flying saucer.

According to information released by the department over the authority of Major J.A. Marcel, intelligence officer, the disk was recovered on a ranch in the Roswell vicinity after an unidentified rancher had notified Sheriff Geo. Wilcox here, that he had found the instrument on his premises.

Major Marcel and a detail from his department went to the ranch and recovered the disk, it was stated.

After the intelligence officer here had inspected the disk it was flown to "higher headquarters."

The intelligence office stated that no details of the saucer's construction or its appearance had been revealed.

Mr. and Mrs. Dan Wilmot apparently were the only persons in Roswell who have seen what they thought was a flying disk.

They were sitting on their porch at 105 South Penn. last Wednesday night at about ten minutes before ten o'clock when a large glowing object zoomed out of the sky from the southeast, going in a northwesterly direction at a high rate of speed.

Wilmot called Mrs. Wilmot's attention to it and both ran down into the yard to watch. It was in sight less than a minute, perhaps 40 or 50 seconds, Wilmot estimated.

A wave of UFO sightings swept Europe in 1954. Here, a London newspaper vendor capitalizes on the public hysteria to sell an issue of the *Picture Post* featuring a photo-fiction story about the coming alien invasion. (Hulton Archive/Getty Images)

Wilmot said it appeared to him to be about 1,500 feet high and going fast. He estimated between 400 and 500 miles per hour.

In appearance it looked oval in shape like two inverted saucers faced mouth to mouth or like two old-fashioned wash bowls placed together in the same fashion. The entire body glowed as though lights were showing through from inside, though not like it would be if a light were merely underneath.

From where he stood Wilmot said the object looked to be about 5 feet in size, and making allowance for the distance it was from town he figured it must have been 15 or 20 feet in diameter, though this was just a guess.

Wilmot said he heard no sound but that Mrs. Wilmot said she heard a swishing sound for a very short time.

The object came into view from the southeast and disappeared over the treetops in the general vicinity of Six-Mile Hill.

Wilmot, who is one of the most respected and reliable citizens in town, kept the story to himself hoping that someone else would come out and tell about having seen one, but finally today decided that he would go ahead and tell about seeing it. The announcement that the RAAF was in possession of one came only a few minutes after he had decided to release the details of what he had seen.

∾

In a crowd every sentiment and act is contagious. And contagious to such a degree that an individual readily sacrifices his personal interest to the collective interest.
—Gustave Le Bon,
The Crowd: A Study of the Popular Mind

James Thurber on the Day
the Dam Broke

Rumor and suggestion often flow together in combustible ways, sometimes by chance, sometimes by design. The art of spin, so practiced by political handlers and corporate public-relations offices and consultants, is mostly just the art of balancing rumor and suggestion in such a way as to keep control of a story while massing public attention toward a prescribed end, whether it's the genius or compassion of the handlers' principal or the stupidity and calumny of his or her critics and enemies.

For Bill Clinton, in the closing years of his presidency, spin meant keeping the Monica Lewinsky story suitably fuzzy at the edges so the public had trouble zeroing in on it. Bill Gates's spin artists used many of the same tactics to blur the outlines during Microsoft's long legal battle with the Justice Department. In the battle over the merger between Hewlett-Packard and Compaq, so much spin was flying that the earth below seemed to have come unhinged from its axis.

But as James Thurber shows in this wonderful moment from his memoir *My Life and Hard Times,* sometimes the intersection of rumor and suggestion can be nothing but funny. Such was the case the day the dam "broke" in Thurber's hometown of Columbus, Ohio.

My memories of what my family and I went through during the 1913 flood in Ohio I would gladly forget. And yet neither the hardships we endured nor the turmoil and confusion we experienced can alter my feeling toward my native state and city. I am having a fine time now and wish Columbus were here, but if anyone ever wished a city was in hell it was during that frightful and perilous afternoon in 1913, when the dam broke, or, to be more exact, when everybody in town thought that the dam broke. We were both ennobled and demoralized by the experience. Grandfather especially rose to magnificent heights which can never lose their splendor for me, even though his reactions to the flood were based upon a profound misconception, namely, that Nathan Bedford Forrest's cavalry was the menace we were called upon to face. The only possible means of escape for us was to flee the house, a step which grandfather sternly forbade, brandishing his old army saber in his hand.

"Let the sons —— come!" he roared. Meanwhile hundreds of people were streaming by our house in wild panic, screaming "Go east! Go east!" We had to stun grandfather with the ironing board. Impeded as we were by the inert form of the old gentleman—he was taller than six feet and weighed almost a hundred and seventy pounds—we were passed, in the first half-mile, by practically everybody else in the city. Had grandfather not come to, at the corner of Parsons Avenue and Town Street, we would unquestionably have been overtaken and engulfed by the roaring waters—that is, if there had been any roaring waters. Later, when the panic had died down and people had gone rather sheepishly back to their homes and their offices, minimizing the distances they had run and offering various reasons for running, city engineers pointed out that even if the dam had broke, the water level would not have risen more than two additional inches in the West Side. The West Side was, at the time of the dam scare, under thirty feet of water—as, indeed, were all Ohio river towns during the great spring floods of twenty years ago. The East Side (where we lived and where all the running occurred) had never been in any danger at all. Only a rise of some ninety-five feet could have caused the flood waters to flow over High Street—the thoroughfare that divided the east side of town from the west—and engulf the East Side.

The fact that we were all as safe as kittens under a cookstove did not, however, assuage in the least the fine despair and the grotesque desperation which seized upon the residents of the East Side when the cry spread like a grass fire that the dam had given way. Some of the most dignified, staid, cynical, and clear-thinking men in town abandoned their wives, stenographers, homes, and offices and ran east. There are few alarms in the world more terrifying than "The dam has broken!" There are few persons capable of stopping to reason when that clarion cry strikes upon their ears, even persons who live in towns no nearer than five hundred miles to a dam.

The Columbus, Ohio, broken-dam rumor began, as I recall it, about noon of March 12, 1913. High street, the main canyon of trade, was loud with the placid hum of business and the buzzing of placid businessmen arguing, computing, wheedling, offering, refusing, compromising. Darius Conningway, one of the foremost corporation lawyers in the Middle-West, was telling the Public Utilities Commission in the language of Julius Caesar that they might as well try to move the Northern star as to move him. Other men were making their little boasts and their little gestures. Suddenly somebody began to run. It may be that he had simply remembered, all of a moment, an engagement to meet his wife, for which he was now frightfully late. Whatever it was, he ran east on Broad Street (probably toward the Maramor Restaurant, a favorite place for a man to meet his wife). Somebody else began to run, perhaps a newsboy in high spirits. Another man, a portly gentleman of affairs, broke into a trot. Inside of ten minutes, everybody on High Street, from the Union Depot to the Courthouse was running. A loud mumble gradually crystallized into the dread word "dam." "The dam has broke!" The fear was put into words by a little old lady in an electric, or by a traffic cop, or by a small boy: nobody knows who, nor does it now really matter. Two thousand people were abruptly in full flight. "Go east!" was the cry that arose—east away from the river, east to safety. "Go east! Go east! Go east!"

Black streams of people flowed eastward down all the streets leading in that direction; these streams, whose headwaters were in the drygoods stores, office buildings, harness shops, movie theaters, were fed by trickles of housewives, children, cripples, servants, dogs, and cats, slipping out of the houses past which the main streams flowed, shouting and screaming. People ran out leaving fires burning and food cooking and doors wide open. I remember, however, that my mother turned out all the fires and that she took with her a dozen eggs and two loaves of bread. It was her plan to make Memorial Hall, just two blocks away, and take refuge somewhere in the top of it, in one of the dusty rooms where war veterans met and where old battle flags and stage scenery were stored. But the seething throngs, shouting "Go east!" drew her along and the rest of us with her. When grandfather regained full consciousness, at Parsons Avenue, he turned upon the retreating mob like a vengeful prophet and exhorted the men to form ranks and stand off the Rebel dogs, but at length he, too, got the idea that the dam had broken and, roaring "Go east!" in his powerful voice, he caught up in one arm a small child and in the other a slight clerkish man of perhaps forty-two and we slowly began to gain on those ahead of us.

A scattering of firemen, policemen, and army officers in dress uniforms—there had been a review at Fort Hayes, in the northern part of town—added color to the surging billows of people. "Go east!" cried a little child in a piping voice, as she ran past a porch on which drowsed a lieutenant-colonel of infantry. Used to quick decisions, trained to immediate obedience, the officer bounded off the porch and, running at full tilt, soon passed the child, bawling "Go east!" The two of them emptied rapidly the houses of the little street they were on. "What is it? What is it?" demanded a fat, waddling man who intercepted the colonel. The officer dropped behind and asked the little child what it was. "The dam has broke!" gasped the girl. "The dam has broke!" roared the colonel. "Go east! Go east!" He was soon leading, with the exhausted child in his arms, a fleeing company of three hundred persons who had gathered around him from living-rooms, shops, garages, backyards, and basements.

Nobody has ever been able to compute with any exactness how many people took part in the great rout of 1913, for the panic, which extended from the Winslow Bottling Works in the south end to Clintonville, six miles north, ended as abruptly as it began and the bob-tail and ragtag and velvet-gowned groups of refugees melted away and slunk home, leaving the streets peaceful and deserted. The shouting, weeping, tangled evacuation of the city lasted not more than two hours in all. Some few people got as far east as Reynoldsburg, twelve miles away; fifty or more reached the Country Club, eight miles away; most of the others gave up, exhausted, or climbed trees in Franklin Park, four miles out. Order was restored and fear dispelled finally by means of militiamen riding about in motor lorries bawling through megaphones: "The dam has not broken!" At first this tended only to add to the confusion and increase the panic, for many stampedes thought the soldiers were bellowing "The dam has now broken!", thus setting an official seal of authentication on the calamity.

All the time, the sun shone quietly and there was nowhere any sign of oncoming waters. A visitor in an airplane, looking down on the straggling, agitated masses of people below, would have been hard

"I'm a sucker for group dynamics."

put to it to divine a reason for the phenomenon. It must have inspired, in such an observer, a peculiar kind of terror, like the sight of the *Marie Celeste,* abandoned at sea, its galley fires peacefully burning, its tranquil decks bright in the sunlight.

An aunt of mine, Aunt Edith Taylor, was in a movie theater on High Street when, over and above the sound of the piano in the pit (a W.S. Hart picture was being shown), there rose the steadily increasing tromp of running feet. Persistent shouts rose about the tromping. An elderly man, sitting near my aunt, mumbled something, got out of his seat, and went up the aisle at a dogtrot. This started everybody. In an instant the audience was jamming the aisles. "Fire!" shouted a woman who always expected to be burned up in a theater; but now the shouts outside were louder and coherent. "The dam has broke!" cried somebody. "Go east!" screamed a small woman in front of my aunt. And east they went, emerging finally into the street, torn and sprawling. Inside the theater, Bill Hart was calmly calling some desperado's bluff and the brave girl at the piano played "Row! Row! Row!" loudly and then "In My Harem." Outside, men were streaming across the Statehouse yard, others were climbing trees, a woman managed to get up onto the "These Are My Jewels" statue, whose bronze figures of Sherman, Stanton, Grant, and Sheridan watched with cold unconcern the going to pieces of the capital city.

"I ran south to State Street, east on State to Third, south on Third to Town, and out east on Town," my aunt Edith has written me. "A tall spare woman with grim eyes and a determined chin ran past me down the middle of the street. I was still uncertain as to what was the matter, in spite of all the shouting. I drew up alongside the woman with some effort, for although she was in her late fifties, she had a beautiful easy running form and seemed to be in excellent condition. 'What is it?' I puffed. She gave me a quick glance and then looked ahead again, stepping up her pace a trifle. 'Don't ask me, ask God!' she said.

"When I reached Grant Avenue, I was so spent that Dr. H.R. Mallory—you remember Dr. Mallory, the man with the white beard who looks like Robert Browning?—well, Dr. Mallory, whom I had drawn away from at the corner of Fifth and Town, passed me. 'It's got us!' he shouted, and I felt sure that whatever it was did have us, for you know what conviction Dr. Mallory's statements always carried. I didn't know at the time what he meant, but I found out later. There was a boy behind him on roller skates, and Dr. Mallory mistook the swishing of the skates for the sound of rushing water. He eventually reached the Columbus School for Girls, at the corner of Parsons Avenue and Town Street, where he collapsed, expecting the cold frothing waters of the Scioto to sweep him into oblivion. The boy on the skates swirled past him and Dr. Mallory realized for the first time what he had been running from. Looking back up the street, he could see no signs of water, but nevertheless, after resting a few minutes, he jogged east again. He caught up with me at Ohio Avenue, where we rested together. I should say that about seven hundred people passed us. A funny thing was that all of them were on foot. Nobody seemed to have had the courage to stop and start his car; but, as I remember it, all cars had to be cranked in those days, which is probably the reason."

The next day, the city went about its business as if nothing had happened, but there was no joking. It was two years or more before you dared treat the breaking of the dam lightly. And even now, twenty years after, there are a few persons, like Dr. Mallory, who will shut up like a clam if you mention the Afternoon of the Great Run.

Keeping Your Head When All About You Are Losing Theirs

The power of rumor and suggestion to move crowds will always be with us. Individually, though, each of us has the choice of whether to join the crowd on its journey. Simply turning the other way whenever a consensus begins to form and the masses start in motion isn't the answer. Some rumors and suggestions, after all, turn out to be true. The milk might really be curdled. The company could, in fact, be heading for a nosedive or the dollar for a pounding on the international currency markets. We ignore all such possibilities at peril to our own well-being. Nor, of course, is going wherever the crowd is going likely to get us anywhere we want to be. The answer lies in between, and as always, that means doing due diligence.

Below, a few rules to keep in mind, culled from experts in the field and time-tested by my own experience.

Evaluate each rumor and suggestion on its own merits, not by the rank of the authority from which it flows. As Richard Kieckhefer, a Northwestern University religion professor and a leading researcher in the witch-hunts of the middle of the last millennium, reminds us: "The interesting historical problems arise when you realize that the witch-hunters were in many cases among the moral and even intellectual leaders of the society."

Beware the power of technology to accelerate the rumor mill and validate its products. "There's a great tendency to give more credence to new technologies," Patricia A. Turner, a folklore professor at the University of California at Davis, told the *Chronicle of Higher Education* in the wake of the September 11, 2001, attack on the World Trade Center. "You get something via e-mail, and it seems to come from a credible-sounding source, so people will believe it and feel obliged to pass it on to someone else."

Beware, also, the natural ego trip that comes with getting inside the rumor mill yourself. "There's a pleasure in passing a rumor along," Professor Turner added. "You've got more power when you're passing it along. It's like when you're a little kid. Remember the taunt, 'I know something you don't know'? . . . That's what's happening."

And never forget Occam's razor, that ancient philosophical tool that slices propositions down to their skeletons. If a rumor comes equipped with too many complications, too many contingencies, too many wrinkles of every shape and size, it's likely to harbor nothing of substance once you pare away the fluff. If it doesn't, there might be something at the core worth listening to.

Finally, keep in mind these seven "laws of crazes" from the American sociologist Edward Alsworth Ross:

- The craze takes time to develop to its height.
- The more extensive its ravages, the stronger the type of intellect that falls prey to it.
- The greater its height, the more absurd the propositions that will be believed or the actions that will be done.
- The higher the craze, the sharper the reaction from it.
- One craze is frequently succeeded by another, exciting emotions of a different character.
- A dynamic society is more craze-ridden than one moving along the ruts of custom.
- Ethnic or mental homogeneity is favorable to the craze.

∿

A rumor is one thing that gets thicker instead of thinner as it is spread.

—Richard Willard Armour

3

FEAR & PANIC

Introduction

Sometimes we can see fear and panic coming almost from the horizon. In wartime, targets—Coventry, Hiroshima, the Taliban mountain stronghold at Tora Bora in Afghanistan—are rarely surprises. The only question is when the bombers will arrive and in what numbers, and what sort of chaos will ensue. Political upheaval in the Middle East produces gas-price chaos for American drivers long before any actual disruption of supply can work its way through the pipeline. In the financial arena, investors often set arbitrary numbers in their own minds: the U.S. gold reserve at $100 million, in the case of the panic of 1893; the Nasdaq average at 2000, in the case of the recent dot-com market panic. Until such levels are reached, fear and panic are mostly potential. Once the levels are breached, both are full born, even though many investors have been around this track again and again.

Other times, a specific outbreak of fear and panic will surprise us even though the root causes are obvious on reflection. Andrew Jackson had run a populist campaign for the presidency, promising to unseat the aristocrats in Washington and install a government truly of, by, and for the people. On March 11, 1829, Old Hickory got his wish, and the people to whom he had appealed came to Washington to see him being inaugurated and to celebrate afterwards at the president's mansion. Margaret Bayard Smith, who was there, described the scene at the White House, where as many as 20,000 revelers descended:

> No arrangements had been made, no police officers placed on duty, and the whole house had been inundated by the rabble mob. We came too late. The President, after having been literally nearly pressed to death and almost suffocated and torn to pieces by the people in their eagerness to shake hands with Old Hickory, had retreated through the back way or south front and had escaped to his lodgings at Gadsby's.
>
> Cut glass and china to the amount of several thousand dollars had been broken in the struggle to get the refreshments. . . . Ladies fainted, men were seen with bloody noses, and such a scene of confusion took place as is impossible to describe—those who got in could not get out by the door again but had to scramble out of windows.
>
> At one time the President, who had treated and retreated until he was pressed against the wall, could only be secured by a number of gentlemen forming round him and making a kind of barrier of their own bodies; and the pressure was so great that Colonel Bomford, who was one, said that at one time he was afraid they should have been pushed down or on the President. It was then the windows were thrown open and the torrent found an outlet, which otherwise might have proved fatal.

Often, fear and panic seem to materialize from the air around us. One moment our life is safe; the next, we're in mortal peril. No one went to work in Lower Manhattan or at the Pentagon on September 11, 2001, thinking the world was about to be turned upside down. When it suddenly and horribly was, the norms we guide ourselves by were all turned on their ear. One Washington woman, nearly eight months pregnant with her first child, tells of leaving her office on Dupont Circle within minutes of the attack on the Pentagon and walking almost 10 miles in heels to her home in suburban Virginia—a commute of less than 30 minutes on the Metro subway system that took her almost four hours by foot. New York City was full of dazed, aimless wanderers in the hours after the attacks there, people

May 30, 1883: A huge throng had turned out for the opening day of the Brooklyn Bridge when someone in the crowd shouted—anonymously and with no basis—that the bridge was about to collapse. A dozen pedestrians were trampled to death during the ensuing panic.

unhurt by the collapse of the World Trade Center towers but fully in the grip of fear and panic all the same.

Sometimes, too, the precipitating event isn't even real. Rumor and the power of suggestion reach a kind of critical mass. The herd instinct is awakened. Our internal alarms go off as surely as if we had seen a fire break out on the stage of a theater in the middle of a show.

In the late 1980s, a high school student in Hazelton, Pennsylvania, took his life without leaving a suicide note. An investigation into the incident never did uncover a reason, but as the probe went on, a rumor spread among the student body that the dead boy had been part of a satanic cult and that he was only its first act. The cult intended to strike again, the rumor held in its final version, this time at an upcoming spring prom. Perhaps its members would poison the punch. Maybe they would open fire on their classmates, or on themselves—a group suicide in the fulfillment of some dictate from their private prince of darkness. Not surprisingly, as prom night grew closer, the rumor turned to fear and the fear, finally, to what Bill Ellis, a professor at Pennsylvania State University at Hazelton, has called "rumor panic."

Fortunately, that's as far as the story goes. There was no incident at the Hazelton prom, no unexplained death to further stoke the fear that had gripped the school. Afterwards, the panic evaporated as quickly as it had formed, but once rumor and the power of suggestion transform themselves into something stronger, the outcome is never predictable.

In 1789, a contagion of fear stole over the small towns and hamlets of rural France in a way strikingly similar, for all the differences in time and detail, to what had happened at the Pennsylvania high school.

"The months of July and August may be called the months of the 'great fear,' " H. Morse Stephens writes in his history of the French Revolution. "Men were afraid, both in town and country, of they knew not what."

By the end of July, Stephens recounts, the fear had crystallized around a rumor that the king was paying brigands to rob the people—not entirely unreasonable given the revolution then raging in Paris and other large cities, but a rumor without a shred of known fact to it. By then, though, the contagion had created an unstoppable momentum.

"At Chateau-Thierry news arrived, on July 28, that 2500 'carabots,' or brigands, were marching along the Soissons road," Stephens writes. "The tocsin sounded, and the bourgeois marched out to meet them. On their way a miller told them that the brigands had just sacked Bouresches, which was in flames; but when the partisans of order arrived there, the flames were found to be only the reflection of the sun upon the roofs of the houses. Then the brigands were described in the act of crossing the Marne at Essommes; but when the tired pursuers came up, they found that these new brigands were the women of Essommes, who had been scared at their appearance and who believed them to be the real brigands."

In effect, the fear had circled around the Frenchmen and bitten them in the *derriere*.

We've all experienced the physical manifestations of fear and panic: a sudden feeling of loss of control, the desire to flee wherever it is we find ourselves at the moment. Blood rushes to the head and heart, the places it's most needed. Muscles are put on alert. In extreme cases—prolonged time underwater, near suffocation from dense smoke—the body begins to shut down, or shunt, at the extremities so it can concentrate on keeping the vital organs alive.

A colleague describes being in an introductory psychology class nearly 40 years ago at the University of Virginia when the professor walked in, reached in his briefcase, pulled out a starter's gun, and immediately fired off six blanks.

"Freeze!" he yelled as the last shot was still reverberating off the lecture hall walls. "Look at yourselves! That's the classic startle reaction."

And indeed it was: eyes wide, pupils dilated, mouth open to increase the flow of oxygen, jaw jutted forward, everyone poised on the edge of their seat, ready for flight or fight. A multimillionaire traveling on the maiden voyage of the *Titanic* would have reacted the same way when the "unsinkable" liner first crashed into the iceberg. So does your pet cat when it hears a sudden loud noise, and so does a giraffe on the African veldt. All across the animal kingdom, fear and panic are the great equalizer.

∾

To act without understanding—that is the way of the mob.

—Mencius, *Discourse*

Worst-Case Scenario: The Martians Are Coming!

On the surface, the sudden outbreak of panic that swept America on the evening of October 30, 1938, makes no sense whatsoever. Spurred on by nothing more than a radio dramatization of H.G. Wells's 1898 space-invasion thriller *War of the Worlds,* people by the thousands took leave of their senses, certain that the fictional Martian attack being broadcast on Orson Welles's *Mercury Theater on the Air* was the real McCoy.

In Newark, New Jersey, *Time* magazine reported in its November 7, 1938, issue, more than 20 families wrapped their faces in wet towels in expectation of an imminent Martian gas attack and 15 people were treated for shock at St. Michael's Hospital alone. In Tennessee, the *Memphis Press-Scimitar* recalled its editorial staff and began to prepare for a special edition on the bombing of Chicago and St. Louis. Memphis itself was said to be threatened. A Pittsburgh man was barely able to stop his wife from swallowing poison after she screamed, "I'd rather die this way than that!" Meanwhile, an extremely punctual Dayton, Ohio, man telephoned the *New York Times* to find out the exact hour when the world would come to an end.

Mercury Theater's "War of the Worlds" broadcast was preceded and followed by disclaimers. What's more, the airing came on Halloween. (Welles told listeners at the end of the show that it was the theater's "own version of dressing up in a sheet . . . and saying Boo!") As if all that weren't warning enough, listeners merely had to spin the radio dial to discover that the rest of the broadcasting industry was blithely ignoring the story of the millennium. That they didn't led *Time* to wonder if simple mass stupidity hadn't been at least partially to blame.

October 1938, though, was no normal time. On October 3rd, the German army had marched into Sudetenland, less than a week after Britain and France had essentially ceded the Czech border area to Hitler. On the 21st, Japanese troops occupied Canton in China. Two days before the Mercury Theater broadcast, the Nazis began expelling German Jews, sending them to Poland and an uncertain fate. *Kristallnacht*—the night-long rampage against Jewish-owned stores and synagogues—would follow in another 11 days. The world was on edge when Orson Welles took to the airwaves with his unreal tale of extraterrestrial attackers. A real

Armageddon was waiting just down the calendar. When you predispose yourself to expect the worst, the worst can arrive from any direction.

This description of the creation and broadcast of the "War of the Worlds" show, and of its aftermath, comes from the late actor John Houseman, a cofounder along with Orson Welles and others of the Mercury Theater.

Five days before the show, [scriptwriter] Howard Koch telephoned. He was in deep distress. After three days of slaving on H.G. Wells's scientific fantasy he was ready to give up. Under no circumstances, he declared, could it be made interesting or in any way credible to modern American ears. Koch was not given to habitual alarmism. To confirm his fears, Annie, our secretary, came to the phone. She was an acid and emphatic girl from Smith College with fine blond hair, who smelled of fading spring flowers. "You can't do it!" she whined. "Those old Martians are just a lot of nonsense. It's all too silly! We're going to make fools of ourselves! Absolute fools!"

For some reason which I do not clearly remember our only possible alternative for that week was a dreary one—*Lorna Doone*. . . . Unable to reach Welles, I called Koch back. I was severe. I taxed him with defeatism. I gave him false comfort. I promised to come up and help.

When I finally got there—around two the next morning—things were better. He was beginning to have fun laying waste the State of New Jersey. Annie had stopped grinding her teeth. We worked all night and through the next day. Wednesday at sunset the script was finished.

Thursday, as usual, Paul Stewart rehearsed the show, then made a record. We listened to it rather gloomily, long after midnight in Orson's room at the St. Regis, sitting on the floor because all the chairs were covered with coils of unrolled and unedited film. We agreed it was a dull show. We all felt its only chance of coming off lay in emphasizing its newscast style—its simultaneous, eyewitness quality.

All night we sat up, spicing the script with circumstantial allusions and authentic detail. Friday afternoon it went over to CBS to be passed by the Network censor. Certain name alterations were

In this 1906 illustration by Alvin Correco for H.G. Wells's novel *War of the Worlds,* Londoners get a close look at the deadly machines and weaponry used by the invading Martian army. Orson Welles's radio dramatization of the novel would cause a national panic in America when aired 32 years later. (© Bettmann/CORBIS)

requested. Under protest and with a deep sense of grievance we changed the Hotel Biltmore to a nonexistent Park Plaza, Trans-America to Intercontinent, the Columbia Broadcasting Building to Broadcasting Building. Then the script went over to mimeograph and we went to bed. We had done our best and, after all, a show is just a show. . . .

Around six we left the studio. Orson, phoning from the theater a few minutes later to find out how things were going, was told by one of the CBS sound men, who had stayed behind to pack up his equipment, that it was not one of our better shows. Confidentially, the man opined, it just didn't come off. . . .

On Sunday, October 30, at 8:00 p.m., E.S.T., in a studio littered with coffee cartons and sandwich paper, Orson swallowed a second container of pineapple juice, put on his earphones, raised his long white fingers and threw the cue for the Mercury theme—the Tchaikovsky Piano Concerto In B Flat Minor # 1. . . .

His sense of tempo, that night, was infallible. When the flashed news of the cylinder's landing finally came—almost fifteen minutes after the beginning of a fairly dull show—he was able suddenly to spiral his action to a speed as wild and reckless as its base was solid. The appearance of the Martians; their first treacherous act; the death of Carl Phillips; the arrival of the militia; the battle of the Watchung Hills; the destruction of New Jersey—all these were telescoped into a space of twelve minutes without ever stretching the listener's emotional credulity. The broadcast, by then, had its own reality, the reality of emotionally felt time and space. . . .

I remember, during the playing of the final theme, the phone starting to ring in the control room and a shrill voice through the receiver announcing itself as belonging to the mayor of some Midwestern city, one of the big ones. He is screaming for Welles. Choking with fury, he reports mobs in the streets of his city, women and children huddled in the churches, violence and looting. If, as he now learns, the whole thing is nothing but a crummy joke—then he, personally, is coming up to New York to punch the author of it on the nose! Orson hangs up quickly. For we are off the air now and the studio door bursts open. The following hours are a nightmare. The building is suddenly full of people and dark blue uniforms. We are hurried out of the studio, downstairs, into a back office. Here we sit incommunicado while network employees are busily collecting, destroying, or locking up all scripts and records of the broadcast. Then the press is let loose upon us, ravening for horror. How many deaths have we heard of? (Implying they know of thousands.) What do we know of the fatal stampede in a Jersey hall? (Implying it is one of many.) What traffic deaths? (The ditches must be choked with corpses.) The suicides? (Haven't you heard about the one on Riverside Drive?) It is all quite vague in my memory and quite terrible.

Hours later, instead of arresting us, they let us out a back way. . . . We were on the front page for two days. Having had to bow to radio as a news source during the Munich crisis, the press was now only too eager to expose the perilous irresponsibilities of the new medium. Orson was their whipping boy. They quizzed and badgered him. Condemnatory editorials were delivered by our press-clipping bureau in bushel baskets. There was talk, for a while, of criminal action.

Then gradually, after about two weeks, the excitement subsided. By then it had been discovered that the casualties were not as numerous or as serious as had at first been supposed. One young woman had fallen and broken her arm running downstairs. . . .

Of the suits that were brought against us—amounting to over three quarters of a million dollars for damages, injuries, miscarriages and distresses of various kinds—none was substantiated or legally proved. We did settle one claim, however, against the advice of our lawyers. It was the particularly affecting case of a man in Massachusetts, who wrote:

"I thought the best thing to do was to go away. So I took three dollars twenty-five cents out of my savings and bought a ticket. After I had gone sixty miles I knew it was a play. Now I don't have money left for the shoes I was saving up for. Will you please have someone send me a pair of black shoes size 9B!"

We did.

~

The masses are governed more by impulse than conviction.

—Wendell Phillips

Nearly 10,000 people, mostly women, tried to force their way into New York City's Campbell Funeral Home in August 1926 for a last look at Rudolph Valentino, the film idol who had died suddenly at age 31. At least a hundred women were injured, many by flying glass as the crowd crushed windows along Broadway. (© Bettmann/CORBIS)

Life Imitates Art,
Art Imitates Life

As the reaction to Orson Welles's "War of the Worlds" broadcast suggests, the line between art and life can be simultaneously wide as a canyon and razor thin. The job of the screenwriter, the novelist, even the event publicist is to make his or her audience experience all the elements of fear and panic—the startled reaction, the sense of flight or fight, the racing heart and pulse—without actually throwing down the book or tearing down the theater. Audiences, though, can be hard to control. Once they suspend disbelief, in Samuel Taylor Coleridge's famous formulation, they are likely to suspend decorum, too, and even sometimes regard for human life. In these two excerpts, one fictional and one nonfiction, we see what happens when the buildup of fear and panic becomes a stampede.

Rudolph Valentino was in his mid-20s when he got his first starring Hollywood role and only 31 when he died, in August 1926 in Manhattan, of peritonitis. Yet so powerful was his screen presence at suggesting a smoldering romantic that at least one woman greeted the news of his passing by shooting herself to death rather than face life without her celluloid lover. Valentino's funeral arrangements were meant to cement his place in the pantheon of movie stars: He would lie in state in New York City, the nation's population locus and home of the most influential news outlets, before being transported to Hollywood for a predictably garish funeral. But somewhere between the plan and its execution, human nature intervened. This account is from J.P. Chaplin's *Rumor, Fear, and the Madness of Crowds*.

On August 24th, 1926, one of the worst riots in the history of New York City erupted on Broadway near 66th Street. Between sixty and eighty thousand persons were involved, hundreds of whom were injured. An emergency hospital had to be set up at the scene of the disturbances to care for those trampled under foot or lacerated by fragments from broken windows. A task force of nearly two hundred policemen was eventually mobilized to bring the mob under control and then only after mounties repeatedly charged the rioters, most of whom were women. The cause of these unruly legions in the heart of

New York City was the dead body of Rudolph Valentino, the greatest movie hero of the day, and possibly of all time. The milling throngs had come to pay their last respects to the dead actor as he lay in state in a Broadway funeral parlor.

The times were ripe for such an outbreak of hysteria. It was an era celebrated for excesses and exhibitionism in every facet of human behavior. The gin of the F. Scott Fitzgeralds set the pace along bibulous lines. Extraordinary public demonstrations of physical prowess were common, and nearly every woman who boasted a good set of muscles and any swimming ability whatever took to the nearest body of water in an attempt to emulate Trudy Ederle's feat of feminine endurance in the English Channel. Those with lesser talents, but an irrepressible urge for the limelight, put on hair-raising deeds of derring-do for no better reason than putting on deeds of derring-do. In cities of any appreciable size, men and women were hauled aloft while dangling from the landing gear of barnstorming airplanes. Others performed tightrope stunts on the edges of roofs on the highest buildings in town. Meanwhile their more dexterous brethren exercised their curious talents by escaping from strait-jackets while suspended head downward eight or ten stories above the streets. There seemed to be no limit to human ingenuity in contriving masterpieces of sheer foolishness.

But however much one might admire marathon parties, macabre murders or super-stuntsters, the real idol of the hour at the mid-point of the Twenties was Rudolph Valentino. His movie love-making gave his female fans high voltage emotional jolts. In person, he was a handsome Latin reported to be worth millions. He could dance with the grace of a ballerina and fence like a musketeer. He won and took to wife an heiress and two glamorous movie actresses in his three unsuccessful experiments with matrimony. Wherever he went he was besieged by adoring flappers, and his mail was full of mash notes. Men, too, came under his spell, and many copied his oiled back hairdo, gaucho-style sideburns and broad-bottomed trousers.

On the 19th, a cruel rumor was spread through the city that Valentino had died. Calls immediately began to pour into the hospital to reach a peak rate of two thousand an hour for over four hours.

Two extra operators were required to handle the load. In some sec-
tions of the city, premature mourning began. Saleswomen in department stores lowered their heads to their counters and sobbed,
unmindful of their bewildered customers. But aside from these
unwarranted developments, there was little else for the papers to pub-
lish on the case.

By the time the funeral parlor opened at four, twelve thousand
people had gathered in the streets in a soaking rain in anticipation of
viewing the remains.

When the doors were opened, the mourners entered in force.
There were stylish flappers, shabbily dressed women with shawls over
their heads, well-dressed matrons in furs, men and boys—all classes,
colors and races. They shuffled past the dead lover for a two-second
look at his emaciated face. Outside, the crowd swelled to an estimated
sixty thousand. The mourners formed a line, in some places four
abreast, which extended for eleven blocks. . . . Time after time the
crowd got out of hand, and mounted police were forced to charge in
order to restore order.

While Valentino was drawing the largest crowd of his career, other
manifestations of the hysteria were going on elsewhere. Inside the
funeral chambers, telephone calls from all points in the nation arrived
at the rate of twenty a minute. Downtown, rumors were circulating
that the body would be interred in a solid bronze coffin weighing a
ton and a half. However, this improbable estimate was subsequently
denied by S. George Ullman. More sinister rumors charging that
Valentino's death had resulted from poisoning gained sufficient credence than an assistant district attorney let it be known he was unable
to take action on such unsubstantial charges. An equally irresponsi-
ble story was circulated to the effect that the squadron of doctors who
had attended the actor were ill as a result of their prolonged vigil.
Finally, the same day, a bulletin arrived over the wire services from the
other side of the nation with the latest intelligence on the condition of
Miss Negri [the famous silent-film star Pola Negri]. She was being
attended by two physicians and two nurses, having suffered a complete nervous collapse when informed of her reputed fiancee's death.

That night when the funeral parlor closed, between sixty and
eighty thousand mourners had passed the remains.

"Damn it, Miss Blake! Who pushed the panic button?"

Finally, the whole business was to a large degree phony from the very beginning. Had the lying in state been conducted with decorum, it would never have attracted such crowds. However, the actor's manager engineered the affair with almost ghoulish skill. The undertaker's press agent provided the newspapers with photographs of the chambers where the dead man would lie and, in addition, gave them posed pictures of the funeral cortege, one of which accidentally got out before the funeral took place. Similarly, the exaggerated newspaper reports of wild grief suffered by the principals and others at the bier, and the long delay between the actor's death and departure for Hollywood added fuel to the fires of madness.

A dozen years after Rudolph Valentino's death, Nathanael West created in his novel *The Day of the Locust* his own version of a crowd driven to madness by Hollywood publicists. Born in New York and based in Hollywood, West had an uncanny feel for both epicenters of the bicoastal hype machine. Here, the novel's central character, painter Tod Hackett, is swept up in a Hollywood crowd waiting in front of a movie theater on opening night for the stars to arrive.

The next thing Tod knew, he was torn loose from Homer and sent to his knees by a blow in the back of the head that spun him sideways. The crowd in front of the theatre had charged. He was surrounded by churning legs and feet. He pulled himself erect by grabbing a man's coat, then let himself be carried along backwards in a long, curving swoop. He saw Homer rise above the mass for a moment, shoved against the sky his jaw hanging as though he wanted to scream but couldn't. A hand reached up and caught him by his open mouth and pulled him forward and down.

There was another dizzy rush. Tod closed his eyes and fought to keep upright. He was jostled about in a hacking cross surf of shoulders and backs, carried rapidly in one direction and then in the opposite. He kept pushing and hitting out at the people around him, trying to face in the direction he was going. Being carried backwards terrified him.

Using the eucalyptus tree as a landmark, he tried to work toward it by slipping sideways against the tide, pushing hard when carried away from it and riding the current when it moved toward his objective. He was within only a few feet of the tree when a sudden, driving rush carried him far past it. He struggled desperately for a moment, then gave up and let himself be swept along. He was the spearhead of a flying wedge when it collided with a mass going in the opposite direction. The impact turned him around. As the two forces ground against each other, he was turned again and again, like a grain between millstones. This didn't stop until he became part of the opposing force. The pressure continued to increase until he thought he must collapse. He was slowly being pushed into the air.

~

If by the people you understand the multitude, the hoi polloi, 'tis no matter what they think: their judgment is a mere lottery.

—John Dryden, *Essay on Dramatic Poetry*

John McClellan, *Panic* (1937)

The Iroquois Theater Fire: "They Had Gone Mad"

Under normal circumstances, the conjunction of panic and fear presents us with a choice: to fight or flee. In the financial markets, that can mean taking a stand as prices are falling on all sides of you, or joining the mob and bailing out of holdings that had seemed perfectly sound only days before. Military commanders face similar moments of truth: to dig in, to beat a retreat, maybe even to surrender. Surely there must have come a moment during the collapse of the energy-trading giant Enron when the partners at Arthur Andersen wondered whether to fight for their firm or flee to the competition. Both responses are human nature.

Fire, though, tends to take panic and people beyond the breaking point. Nothing excites our animal instincts more than fire because nothing assaults our senses on more fronts simultaneously. There's the intense heat, the burning smell. If the smoke is heavy, we're denied sight. Fire also changes the very composition of the air we breathe by sucking the oxygen out of it and converting it to more fuel and even greater heat.

Outdoors, the response to a raging fire is almost universal. Whether we're deer in a burning woods or mice or people caught by a raging grass fire, we run at top speed away from the source. Indoors, all our instincts tell us to do the same, but with far more dire results. Fear and flight merge with limited access to escape routes to heighten the panic, and the greater the panic, the less reasonable our instinctive and collective behavior becomes.

Perhaps the most famous indoor fire of twentieth-century America is the one that took place on November 28, 1942, at the Cocoanut Grove nightclub in Boston. Some 800 people were inside the club when the fire broke out, and inevitably virtually all of them headed immediately for the revolving-door exit.

"Flames flashed with incredible swiftness," *Newsweek* wrote in its December 7, 1942, account of the catastrophe. "Smoke swirled in choking masses through hallways. The revolving doors jammed as the terror-stricken mob pushed them in both directions at the same time. Blazing draperies fell, setting women's evening gowns and hair on fire. Patrons were hurled under tables and trampled to death. Others tried and choked the 6-foot-wide stairway up from the Melody Lounge. Those behind swarmed over them and piled up in layers—layers of corpses."

Of the 800 patrons caught in the club, only 10 escaped unharmed, and half of those were employees familiar with alternate exits. Just shy of 500 people would die in the fire, making it the second most deadly theater fire in American history. The worst such fire occurred 39 years earlier, on December 30, 1903, at the Iroquois Theater in Chicago. Like the Cocoanut Grove fire, the Iroquois one was quickly brought under control but with a devastating loss of life—ultimately more than 600 people.

The comedian Eddie Foy was performing at the Iroquois that night. He described it thus in *Clowning through Life,* his 1928 autobiography written with Alvin F. Harlow.

As I ran around back of the rear drop, I could hear the murmur of excitement growing in the audience. Somebody had of course yelled "Fire!"—there is almost always a fool of that species in an audience; and there are always hundreds of people who go crazy the moment they hear the word. The crowd was beginning to surge toward the doors and already showing signs of a stampede. Those on the lower floor were not so badly frightened as those in the more dangerous balcony and gallery. Up there they were falling into panic.

I began shouting at the top of my voice, "Don't get excited. There's no danger. Take it easy!" And to Dillea, the orchestra leader, "Play, start an overture—anything! But play!" Some of his musicians were fleeing, but a few, and especially a fat little violinist, stuck nobly.

I stood perfectly still, hoping my apparent calm would have an equally calming effect on the crowd. Those on the lower floor heard me and seemed somewhat reassured. But up above, and especially in the gallery, they had gone mad.

As I left the stage, the last of the ropes holding up the drops burned through, and with them the whole loft collapsed with a terrifying crash, bringing down tons of burning material. With that, all the lights in the house went out and another great balloon of flame leaped out into the auditorium, licking even the ceiling and killing scores who had not yet succeeded in escaping from the gallery.

The horror in the auditorium was beyond all description. There were thirty exits, but few of them were marked by lights; some had heavy portieres over the doors, and some of the doors were locked or fastened with levers which no one knew how to work.

It was said that some of the exit doors ... were either rusted or frozen. They were finally burst open, but precious moments had been lost—moments which meant death for many behind those doors. The fire-escape ladders could not accommodate the crowd, and many fell or jumped to death on the pavement below. Some were not killed only because they landed on the cushion of bodies of those who had gone before.

But it was inside the house that the greatest loss of life occurred, especially on the stairways leading down from the second balcony. Here most of the dead were trampled or smothered, though many jumped or fell over the balustrade to the floor of the foyer. In places on the stairways, particularly where a turn caused a jam, bodies were piled seven or eight feet deep. Firemen and police confronted a sickening task in disentangling them. An occasional living person was found in the heaps, but most of these were terribly injured. The heel prints on the dead faces mutely testified to the cruel fact that human animals stricken by terror are as mad and ruthless as stampeding cattle. Many bodies had the clothes torn from them, and some had the flesh trodden from their bones.

Never before had such a disaster occurred so quickly. In just eight minutes, from the start of the fire until all lay dead, injured, or had escaped, more than 500 people perished.

The fire department arrived quickly after the alarm and extinguished the flames in the auditorium so promptly that no more than the plush upholstery was burned off the seats. But when a fire chief thrust his head through a side exit and shouted, "Is anybody alive in here?" no one answered.

∼

The blind monster, with uncounted heads,
The still discordant, wavering multitude.

—Shakespeare

The Mechanics of Disintegration

Individual manifestations of fear and panic are both common and potentially devastating. Everyone wakes up some time or another in the middle of the night, in a cold sweat, terrified of something named or unnamed. Phobias and anxiety and panic attacks are not only more concentrated expressions of everyday fear; they also can be debilitating. It's in crowds, though, that fear and panic find their multiplier effect. The fears of separate individuals play on one another and, in the process, grow exponentially in magnitude. Panic begets wider panic. "Things fall apart," William Butler Yeats wrote at the start of "The Second Coming." "The center cannot hold." That's what happens when fear and panic get loose in a crowd. This study of how a crowd disintegrates under high stress is taken from *Crowds and Power,* by Elias Canetti.

Panic in a theatre, as has often been noted, is a disintegration of the crowd. The more people were bound together by the performance and the more closed the form of the theatre which contained them, the more violent the disintegration.

It is also possible that the performance alone was not enough to create a genuine crowd. The audience may have remained together, not because they felt gripped by it, but simply because they happened to be there. What the play could not achieve is immediately achieved by a fire. Fire is as dangerous to human beings as it is to animals; it is the strongest and oldest symbol of the crowd. However little crowd feeling there may have been in the audience, awareness of a fire brings it suddenly to a head. The common unmistakable danger creates a common fear. For a short time the audience becomes something like a real crowd. If they were not in a theatre, people could flee together like a herd of animals in danger, and increase the impetus of their flight by the simultaneity of identical movements. An active crowd-fear of this kind is the common collective experience of all animals who live together in herds and whose joint safety depends on their speed.

In a theatre, on the other hand, the crowd inevitably disintegrates in the most violent manner. Only one or two persons can get through each exit at a time and thus the energy of flight turns into an energy of struggle to push others back. Only one man at a time can pass between the rows of seats and each seat is neatly separated from the rest. Each man has his place and sits or stands by himself. A normal theatre is arranged with the intention of pinning people down and allowing them only the use of their hands and voices; their use of their legs is restricted as far as possible.

The sudden command to flee which the fire gives is immediately countered by the impossibility of any common movement. Each man sees the door through which he must pass; and he sees himself alone in it, sharply cut off from all the others. It is the frame of a picture which very soon dominates him. Thus the crowd, a moment ago at its apex, must disintegrate violently, and the transmutation shows itself in violent individual action: everyone shoves, hits and kicks in all directions.

The more fiercely each man "fights for his life," the clearer it becomes that he is fighting against all the others who hem him in. They stand there like chairs, balustrades, closed doors, but different from these in that they are alive and hostile. They push him in this or that direction, as it suits them or rather, as they are pushed themselves. Neither women, children nor old people are spared: They are not distinguished from men. Whilst the individual no longer feels himself as "crowd," he is still completely surrounded by it. Panic is a disintegration of the crowd within the crowd. The individual breaks away and wants to escape from it because the crowd, as a whole, is endangered but, because he is physically still stuck in it, he must attack it. To abandon himself to it now would be his ruin, because it itself is threatened by ruin. In such a moment a man cannot insist too strongly on his separateness. Hitting and pushing, he evokes hitting and pushing; and the more blows he inflicts and the more he receives, the more himself he feels.

~

The mob is man voluntarily descending to the nature of the beast.

—Ralph Waldo Emerson, *Compensation*

The last hours of the Vietnam War: An American punches a man trying to board an airplane already overloaded with refugees fleeing Nha Trang. (© Bettmann/CORBIS)

The Fall of Saigon:
"If You Have Time, Pray for Us"

Crowd disintegration is all around us: at the discount store when a "sale" announcement converts a formerly placid herd into every shopper for him- or herself, on the subway platform when commuters rush pell-mell for the opening train doors, or on the floor of the New York Stock Exchange when a buying or selling panic takes the usual orderly process of bids and offers and turns it on its ear. So long as everyone in a crowd waits his or her turn, things are fine, but let one person break from the queue and begin acting on his or her own, and others are certain to follow in a mounting crush. That's when the trouble begins.

For Baby Boom Americans, one of the most poignant examples of crowd disintegration came in April 1975 when the protracted war in Vietnam finally came to an inglorious end. With the North Vietnamese army and its Vietcong allies closing in on Saigon, rumors began to circulate in the South Vietnamese capital of atrocities the conquerors were planning to commit. In the seemingly unbreakable cycle of such events, the rumors fed fears that had already been brought to a boil, and the fears led to a mounting hysteria. Reporter Fox Butterfield filed this story—a classic study of panic and a memorable moment in history—for the April 24, 1975, *New York Times*. Saigon fell to the Communists four days later.

Saigon, South Vietnam, Thursday, April 24—Panic is clearly visible in Saigon now as thousands of Vietnamese try desperately to find ways to flee their country.

There are few exits left, and most involve knowing or working for Americans. United States Air Force C-141 jet transports took off all day and night from the Tan Son Nhut air base, the lucky passengers heading for Clark Air Base in the Philippines or for Andersen Air Force Base on Guam.

Others, not so lucky, rushed to drug stores to buy quantities of sleeping pills and tranquilizers, with which they could commit suicide if the worst came to pass.

Still others, trying to get a seat aboard one of the planes, offered everything they had.

A young American-trained economist who works for the Deputy Premier in charge of economic development asked an American friend to marry his wife, who is three months pregnant, and take her to the United States with him. "I will pay you $10,000," the Vietnamese said.

Under South Vietnam's stringent emigration law, about the only legal way for a citizen to go abroad since the Communist offensive began last month is to be married to a foreigner.

A South Vietnamese Army captain succeeded in getting his young son aboard an American plane by forging a birth certificate and persuading a Vietnamese neighbor who was a secretary in the American Defense Attache's Office to take him as her son. The office has been evacuating its Vietnamese employees for a week and the embassy is doing the same today.

The captain later asked an American acquaintance to mail a letter to his sister, who is married to a former G.I. in Lodi, N.J. "Please take care of my son," he wrote. "Quan is the last drop of blood in our family. If you have time, pray for us."

∾

One will rarely err if extreme actions be ascribed to vanity, ordinary actions to habit, and mean actions to fear.
—Friedrich Wilhelm Nietzsche,
Human, All Too Human

"Back to Square One!"

Russell Baker:
Roar of the Crowd, Inc.

As we've seen in this section, crowds are by nature unstable. Easily led, they have a way of breaking through the boundaries we try to set for them. A sudden startle launches an outbreak of fear. The fear feeds off itself, ascends in scale, and lets loose a collective panic. Before anyone knows it, the exits are blocked, windows are being smashed, beer bottles are raining down on the hapless referee who made the questionable call that startled the crowd into action.

Get rid of the crowd, and you'd get rid the problem, but you'd also lose the sense of excitement a crowd generates. All crowds aren't bad. They create markets and political movements. Crowds give us a sense of belonging: There's something about watching a baseball game with 45,000 other fans that can never be replicated by watching it on a television, no matter how big the screen or how sophisticated the sound system. When crowds arrive in sufficient numbers at sporting events, day in and day out, they can revitalize decaying downtown areas: Baltimore's Inner Harbor offers one excellent example. Crowds can even excite us when they're not physically constituted in a single place. Part of the fun of buying and selling stocks is knowing that we're taking part in a vast global dance of capital.

The problem isn't crowds per se. The problem is the tendency of crowds to get out of hand. In this "modest proposal" from his "Sunday Observer" column in the June 19, 1983, *New York Times,* essayist and humorist Russell Baker offers up a tongue-in-cheek solution to out-of-control crowds that would, alas, bring the problem right back where it started from.

The crowd is obsolete. It impedes traffic and is hard to feed. It is a nuisance to everyone in its vicinity. It is costly to police budgets and, because it creates great quantities of trash and garbage, costly to sanitation budgets.

It is also extremely uncomfortable for its members. They are exposed to shoving, crushing, kicking and trampling. They have only a very poor view or no view at all of the event that causes the crowd to assemble.

Before television, the crowd was necessary. It provided the only mechanism through which the public could hope to catch a glimpse of hangings, campaigning politicians, triumphant heroes, entertainments, fireworks displays and celebratory exercises like the 100th birthday party for the Brooklyn Bridge.

Thanks to television, these great moments can now be enjoyed by millions without the public nuisance, personal discomfort and inadequate views which made the crowd such a burden to everyone. As the crowd begins to vanish from American culture, however, new problems will result.

For example: Much of the pleasure of watching the march of history on television derives from the sight and sound of the crowd surrounding it. When there is no crowd to roar, no crowd to line the streets, no crowd to rock the stadium with their jeers, no angry crowd to cheer the burning of the mayor in effigy, our great occasions will seem only half complete.

To fill this vacuum we shall have the artificial crowd. The simplest form will be the canned crowd. The canned crowd will be the visual equivalent of canned laughter, which situation comedies use to call attention to their laugh lines by inserting recordings of people laughing long ago.

The canned crowd will work on the same principle, interspersing great events with old film of crowds going wild at the 1965 Rose Bowl, the 1968 renomination of Richard Nixon, or whatever may be appropriate.

This cut-rate solution to the crowd problem will not do, however, for many events. Hence, we shall see the rise of the professional crowd, composed of highly skilled graduates of Crowd School, each graduate a master of some specialized skill.

Imagine, for example, that television wants to dramatize the discontent of a group demonstrating at City Hall because its car axles are being shattered by unpatched potholes. At present, TV cameras and lights must be sent to City Hall in hope that the malcontents will become sufficiently inflamed by hopes of appearing on television to create uproar and turmoil.

Football hooliganism came to a tragic head at Heysel Stadium, in Brussels, during the May 29, 1985, European Cup Final between Liverpool and Juventus, of Turin. A series of scuffles among fans, like the one shown here, escalated until a large crowd of Liverpool supporters charged into a solid mass of Juventus rooters just as a wall of the stadium gave way. In all, 39 people were killed and hundreds injured. (Hulton Archive/Getty Images)

Sometimes it works, sometimes it doesn't. Even when it does, the crowd often looks pathetically sparse and its roars of outrage sound sadly forced. Sometimes of course, it gets out of hand and makes a civic mess.

With professional Crowd School graduates, there will be no misfires. The requisite number of professionals, holding degrees in Angry Demonstrating, will be delivered neatly by truck at the fixed time, will give a persuasive performance of snarling and fist-shaking, will chant professionally written slogans and will depart in orderly fashion, having picked up all their litter, in time for the evening news shows.

A less specialized example of the need for professional crowds occurs in sports, where a highly prejudiced crowd of 60,000 or so is required to exhort the home team, abuse the visitors and create the so-called "home-field advantage."

Obviously no sane person will wish to attend such an affair once he learns he can see it better and more comfortably at home. Just as obviously, watching at home will not be much fun without a roaring crowd in the stadium.

To hold the home audience, the television industry, which finances most sports already, will have to hire a professional crowd, highly trained in such specialties as heaving bottles at visiting athletes and toilet paper into the arena.

Yes, hiring professional crowds on this scale will cost money. It will inevitably put athletes in competition with the crowds for a share of the profits.

Labor hostility between players and crowds will surely become intense, leading perhaps to strikes in which the athletes will picket the stadium while 60,000 hired fans sit inside earning their pay by cheering an empty arena.

I can also imagine the anger that might follow such a strike, with enraged athletes and infuriated professional crowdsmen going at each other with fists and feet, bottles and toilet paper. What an improvement in entertainment values over most televised sports of today.

∽

The crowd is always caught by appearance, and the crowd is all there is in the world.
                                        —Machiavelli, *The Prince*

Harry Truman on the
"Harvest of Shame":
What Hysteria Does to Us

Just as exhaustion suppresses our physical immune system and opens us up to cold, viruses, and worse, so fear suppresses our moral immune system and leaves us vulnerable to modes of thought we would reject in healthier times. Fear of economic collapse, of social decline, of governmental failure—all of them can drive us to uncharitable, even cruel acts as surely as the panic induced by a fire can drive us to abandon normal civility in the quest for the nearest exit.

For demagogues, fear is the most fertile soil. Recognizing the anxiety of his audience, the demagogue gives it a magnetic pole to gravitate toward—some cause or specific villain—then harvests the emotion that gathers there. Suddenly, what had been a vague sense of fear passes through panic into mass hysteria, and the streets are bright with torches.

In this 1954 address, Harry S Truman warned of the danger that unchecked fear poses to our fundamental liberties, especially when directed by unscrupulous hands. More directly, he warns both against communism and against the witch-hunts for supposed communist sympathizers that had been undertaken in the Senate by Wisconsin's Joseph McCarthy and by the House Unamerican Activities Committee. President Truman's speech was delivered at Westminster College in Fulton, Missouri—the same venue where Winston Churchill proclaimed eight years earlier that an "Iron Curtain" had rung down over Eastern Europe.

I am particularly mindful, as I recall Churchill's appearance here of the tradition and background of law which is the common basis of our two democracies. It is from the British that we have inherited the concept that a man is innocent until he is proven guilty.

Today crude and sinister men are trying to destroy this concept, and to shake the very foundations of our freedom based on the due process of law. Witch-hunters are on the loose again, often cloaked with immunity, and armed with subpoenas and the cruel whiplash of unevaluated gossip.

In 1950, Wisconsin Senator Joseph McCarthy attracted adoring fans and launched an outbreak of national hysteria with his communist witch-hunts. (AP/Wide World Photo)

History is filled with examples of temporary mob excitement, stirred by false or exaggerated charges, resulting in injury to innocent people. On various occasions, down through the years, mass hysteria has gripped the populace for temporary periods, resulting in a witch hunt.

There is a common pattern in the development of this hysteria.

Usually it takes root in an atmosphere of war, severe economic crisis, or a threat of either. Insecurity is a fruitful breeding ground for such a movement.

In an atmosphere of this kind demagogues or other unprincipled individuals can more easily stir up emotional and irrational fear.

Charges are hurled indiscriminately to an extent that they are directed at obviously innocent individuals. Frequently some of the precious civil rights for which men have fought for centuries are thrown to the winds in the wild effort to make some of the charges stick.

Ignorance and superstition are the principal tools of demagogues as they attempt to inflame mob excitement.

Racial, religious and class animosities are stirred up to add fuel to the flame. Smear attacks are directed against individuals who are the staunchest advocates of liberal and progressive principles. . . .

Mob hysteria broke out into overt attacks on Catholics, such as the burning and pillaging of the Ursuline Convent at Charlestown, Massachusetts; riots in Boston; the tarring and feathering of Catholic priests; the wrecking of a Catholic church in Manchester, New Hampshire; and riots against Catholic workers on the Baltimore and Ohio Railroad and on the Chesapeake and Ohio Canal. All of the mob actions were a prelude to the more widely organized political activities of the anti-Catholics. . . .

The spirit of Know-Nothingism came to life again after World War One. Fear of foreigners and fear of organized labor were manipulated and brought together in the radical scare of the twenties, and in the revival of the Ku Klux Klan. Here again fear was stirred up for political purposes. Educational institutions were attacked. The Catholic religion and the Jewish religion were slandered and vilified. As a result, in many states the Ku Klux Klan rose to considerable political importance.

The Klan, like those other hate movements, was ultimately wiped out by the common sense of the American people. . . .

Once again we are witnessing the return of the political bogeymen who proclaim themselves custodians of our freedom. They are making a mockery of the very institutions they so callously pretend they are seeking to preserve.

They have no more respect for the due process of law and order than the communists they say they hate but whose methods they copy. These descendants of the ancient order of witch-hunters have learned nothing from history. They care nothing for history. They care less for the American traditions of law and order and fair play.

There is even one among them whose torrent of wild charges is calculated to damage the faith of Americans in the integrity of their government, army, schools, churches, their labor unions, and the

Jose Clemente Orayco, *The Masses* (1935) (The Museum of Modern Art, New York, Inter-American Fund. Photograph © 2002 The Museum of Modern Art, New York.)

press. Most of all he is threatening to undermine the respect and confidence Americans must have in one another.

The cause of freedom both at home and abroad is damaged when a great country yields to hysteria.

The way for us to spread democracy is to practice it ourselves.

❧

I have sworn upon the altar of god eternal hostility against every form of tyranny over the mind of man.
                                        —Thomas Jefferson

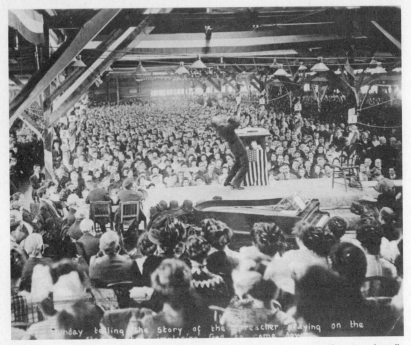

One sure way to attract a crowd: Define an enemy and give them no quarter. The evangelist Billy Sunday, shown in full throttle at a 1920s revival meeting, loved to rail against the "jelly-spined, pussy-footing, four-flushing" Christians attracted by liberal theology.

❦

The devout are always asked to seek truths with their hearts, not their minds.

—Eric Hoffer

Keeping Your Head When All About You Are Losing Theirs

None of us knows how he will react in the grip of fear and panic. Faced with impending disaster, he-men go soft in the knees, and 99 pound weaklings rise to heroic acts. Male or female, powerful or meek, we all experience a rush of adrenaline in an emergency, but how we use that adrenaline—to save ourselves or to save others, to make matters better or worse—is extraordinarily individualistic. The literature of crises is as filled with grandmothers who lifted cars off their grandchildren as it is with thugs who turned tail and ran.

Part of the problem is that it's so hard to train for the moment. Safety manuals can give us the facts and figures and basic stratagems we need: Stay low in a fire; tread water until help comes; press hard on a wound to stem the flow of blood; and so on. But when the actual moment arrives, we find ourselves flushed with emotions we never before experienced and faced with circumstances—too much smoke, water that's too cold to survive in for long, too much blood—that the manuals never can duplicate.

Part of the problem, too, is that the best reaction in a crisis is sometimes the one that doesn't serve the common weal. If a fire breaks out in an enclosed space, the greatest good for the greatest number of people is achieved by filing out the nearest exit, single file, in an orderly fashion, just as we all learned in grade school. Studies, though, show that the people most likely to survive a burning theater or airplane are the ones who ignore order and immediately barrel directly over the seats and heads of their fellows. Comedy for them, as the old saying goes; tragedy for the others.

What's needed in a crisis of fear and panic? Given all the variables, raw good luck doesn't hurt, but here are three ways to tilt the odds in your favor when everything seems to be going to hell around you.

- Make a counterintuitive effort to keep calm. This is easier said than done, of course, and it's easier for some people than for others. The sort of breath control that yoga teaches helps to lower blood pressure so that other natural chemical sedatives can kick in to your system. (Take 10 slow, deep breaths in and out right now, and you'll see how well it works.) Analyzing the situation even as it disintegrates around you also can help. Is there another way out? Is the crisis likely to pass so quickly that inaction is superior to misaction? The stock market teaches us time and again that just because the crowd has arrived at a common answer doesn't mean it's the best answer. Rose Freedman survived the infamous 1911 fire at New York's Triangle Shirtwaist Company not by trying to get down from the 9th floor—the stairs were jammed solid with her fellow workers—but by walking up to the 10th floor, the top floor where the executives had their offices. From there she exited on to the roof and was helped to an adjacent building. Nearly 150 of her colleagues died in the blaze; Freedman lived to be 107.

- Stay detached. Safety experts say that the best way to avoid getting trampled by a crowd is to bring your knees up to your chest and encircle them with your arms. In effect, you're making a small capsule of yourself, a kind of space pod that can roll with the crush or bob above it, rather than get caught underfoot. So it is psychologically, too. The more you can separate yourself in your own mind from the crowd—even if you're forced physically to move with it—the more you will be able to substitute your judgment for the judgment of the whole.

- Cultivate a strong inner compass. Odysseus had the right idea. Knowing that he was about to pass by the isle of the Sirens and fearful that he would succumb to their seductive song, he had his men lash him to the mast of his boat so he wouldn't sail to his doom. In times of crisis, with fear and panic on all sides of us, we need a powerful inner mooring to direct us inside the storm and to help us trust in our own judgment. Borrow from everyone else's bearings, and you will go only where everyone else goes. Know what matters to you, and you'll have the strength of character to go your own way. Sometimes, that's what survival requires.

～

I do not believe in the collective wisdom of individual ignorance.

—Thomas Carlyle

VIOLENCE & VIGILANTES

Introduction

We human beings like to think we aspire to the best models available to us: the wisdom of Solomon, the charity of Mother Teresa, the patience of Gandhi. When Benjamin Franklin set out on a bold course of self-improvement sometime about 1730, he listed 13 virtues he wanted to aspire to: temperance ("Eat not to dullness; drink not to elevation"), silence ("Speak not but what may benefit others or yourself; avoid trifling conversation") order, resolution, and so on. For the 13th and final virtue, humility, he provided this simple description: "Imitate Jesus and Socrates." Franklin recounts in his autobiography that he was striving for moral perfection. Most of us reach for less, but we hope that our individual instincts will lead us naturally to the good.

Crowds tend by their very nature to defeat such lofty goals. Personal aspirations and standards are replaced by groupthink. The norms of behavior are determined collectively, not individually. Instead of sacrificing for future rewards, crowds are impelled by whatever has excited them most recently. Stimulus/response: That's a crowd, as if every one of its members was living together in the salivary glands of Pavlov's famous dog.

Near the end of the 2001 National Football League regular season, Cleveland Browns fans reacted to a questionable penalty call by pelting the field with beer bottles and other makeshift missiles, causing the referees to clear the field for half an hour before the game with Jacksonville could be completed. The next day—a showcase Monday night game in New Orleans between the Saints and St. Louis Rams—a hardcore of Saints fans reacted similarly during the fourth quarter when a call went against their team. One of those arrested for the incident, a 61-year-old roofer, explained his behavior thus to the *New Orleans Times-Picayune:*

"I didn't start it, but I just kind of got caught up in the moment. There were beer bottles flying, and there were two or three by my feet. I said, 'Hey, why not?' Next thing I know, some guard's got me by the arm."

That's the worst of crowd mentality boiled down to its essence: Excitability meets opportunity, just at the moment when a handy target presents itself and a previous incident provides a model for expression. Happily for the referees, players, and others on the field at the New Orleans Superdome, the roofer and his fellow hurlers had beer bottles at hand, not Molotov cocktails. The subjects of a mob's wrath aren't always so fortunate.

The word "riot" comes from the Old French *riote,* meaning a quarrel or dispute, but *riote* itself traces back to *ruire,* "to roar," and so it is with crowds and riots. The group picks, or is led to, a quarrel; the quarrel turns into a roar; and the roar to violence.

Legally, the definition of a "riot" is rooted in English law, expressed in Hawkins's *Pleas of the Crown* as follows:

"A tumultuous disturbance of the peace by three or more persons assembling together of their own authority with an intent mutually to assist one another against any one who shall oppose them in the execution of some enterprise of a private nature and afterwards actually executing the same in a violent and turbulent manner to the terror of the people, and this whether the act intended be of itself lawful or unlawful."

History gets to determine what is a riot and what is not. The destruction of 342 cases of tea in Boston Harbor on the night of December 18, 1773, comes down to us as the Boston Tea Party, not the Boston Tea Riot, in part because for all the violence against property caused by the 200 or so men in Indian disguises who executed the attack, the only person to suffer violence was one of their own: a renter of horses who was caught stuffing his clothing with tea, stripped naked, and coated with mud. But it was the subsequent American victory in the war for independence from Great Britain that assured that Samuel Adams and the others who dumped the tea that night would go down in history as patriots, not hooligans.

Like the Boston Tea Party, riots often are built on a platform of legitimate or, at least, perceived grievances. The 1886 Haymarket Riot in Chicago, one of the bloodiest in American history, grew out of a strike at the McCormick Reaper Company. On April 30, one of the strikers died in a fight with police. The next day, May 1, a bomb thrown at a rally in Haymarket Square to protest the death killed 7 policemen, wounded another 60, and the riot was on. Subsequently, four of the rally leaders would be executed and a fifth would commit suicide while awaiting execution.

The race riots that swept urban America in the 1960s grew out of the whole history of the country, just as the Rodney King riots in Los Angeles were inseparable from the history of race relations in that city. Once violence gets loose in a crowd, though, and once the members set their individual standards aside and assume group norms, causes real or imagined tend to get lost. "Blood will have blood," a weary Macbeth says, tallying up the slaughter. So it is with riots: Violence begets violence in a cascade of unintended consequences.

In the days following the March 5, 1968, assassination of Martin Luther King Jr., more than 30 people died in rioting in Chicago, Baltimore, Cincinnati, and Washington, D.C., where fires set by rioters reached to within blocks of the Capitol. Not only was an apostle of nonviolence honored in death by an orgy of mob violence, looting, and burning; those who suffered the most damage were the inner-city residents King sought to help, along with the small businesses that served the local economy. In a state of riot, mobs have no moral compass, nor any capacity for reason.

As a general rule, the more diffuse the target of a mob, the less violence it rises to. Crowds demonstrate against a government they disagree with. They riot, though, against specific governmental actions: the import tax on tea that led to the Boston Tea Party, the arrest of dissidents that led to the 1989 Tiananmen Square upheaval in China.

Like sunlight, anger grows in destructive force the more it is concentrated. Focus it on specific groups, and anger will burst into flames. Cloak the crowd that contains such anger in the darkness of night or in the artificial darkness of a hood, and the violence gains a further multiplier effect. In a crowd, we lose our individual identity; made anonymous, we gain a license to be someone else entirely. Darkness is the natural milieu of the mob, the time when vigilantes come out to play.

The first vigilantes to be known by that name were members of the vigilance committees established in the small outposts of frontier America to supplement and even supplant existing law authorities. On the sometimes lawless plains of the Old West, there was arguably a logic for enlisting such citizen-policemen. More than one western has glorified the simple shopkeepers who rose up to reclaim their town from outlaws and corrupt sheriffs. But handing over the keys of the law to the crowd always risks substituting passion for reason, rumor for evidence, and score settling for justice. One man's vigilance committee is another man's Ku Klux Klan, and the line that connects vigilantes hanging a cattle rustler to the Klan lynching an innocent black man in Mississippi runs straight and true.

As we'll see later in this section, Mark Twain wrote in *Huck Finn* one of the most memorable fictional accounts of the mind of a lynch mob, but Twain also took on the matter in an essay titled "The United States of Lyncherdom," written at the turn of the century when Twain was in his sixties.

"Why does a crowd . . . in Texas, Colorado, Indiana stand by, smitten to the heart and miserable, and by ostentatious outward signs pretend to enjoy a lynching?" Twain writes. "Why does it lift no hand or voice in protest? Only because it would be unpopular to do it, I think; each man is afraid of his neighbor's disapproval—a thing which, to the general run of the race, is more dreaded than wounds and death. When there is to be a lynching the people hitch up and come miles to see it, bringing their wives and children. Really to see it? No—they come only because they are afraid to stay at home, lest it be noticed and offensively commented upon."

Added to the desire to be accepted, Twain contends, is an equally powerful imitative force that runs through the whole species. A child, he writes, would know that "communities, as well as individuals, are imitators, and that a much-talked-of lynching will infallibly produce other lynchings here and there and yonder, and that in time these will breed a mania, a fashion; a fashion which will spread wide and wider, year by year, covering state after state, as with an advancing disease. Lynching has reached

Colorado, it has reached California, it has reached Indiana, and now Missouri! I may live to see a negro burned in Union Square, New York, with fifty thousand people present, and not a sheriff visible, not a governor, not a constable, not a colonel, not a clergyman, not a law-and-order representative of any sort."

Mark Twain's outrage also hints at what lies on the far, dark side even of lynching. When passions rule, when the rule of law disappears, when states sanction and abet mob rule by word or by deed, when individuals abandon their own moral polestars and adopt the morals of the crowd, rumor abounds, and suggestion assumes an ungodly might. That's when genocide waits in the wings.

∼

There is no grievance that is a fit object of redress by mob law.

—Abraham Lincoln

Los Angeles,
April 29 to May 1, 1992:
Dance of Destruction

When a crowd gets angry enough, when it feels sufficiently aggrieved, sense often steps back into the shadows and retribution takes its place. Corporations often feel the sting in the courtroom: Angry employees will bring suit over work conditions or underfunded pension plans, or angry consumers will go after a company for what are perceived to be slipshod products or neglectful quality control. Ford and Firestone both felt the crowd's rage in the wake of multiple accidents involving Ford Explorers. Sometimes, too, investors will punish stocks not for bad business practices but for what is seen to be bad citizenship. The more irrational the wrath vented on share price, the better the buying opportunity.

It's when an angry crowd runs out of legal recourses for venting its rage—or when it perceives itself powerless in the face of higher authority—that retribution can turn violent. Thus was the case in Los Angeles in the spring of 1992. A year earlier, on March 3, 1991, Rodney King and a passenger, Bryant Allen, were driving on a Los Angeles street when a police car signaled them to stop. Instead, King led police on a nearly eight-mile chase at speeds of up to 100 miles an hour. When King's car finally came to a halt, four policeman beat him viciously for two minutes—56 baton blows and six kicks by actual count. As they worked King over, a man standing on a nearby balcony, George Holliday, captured the scene on a videotape that was soon being played on television stations worldwide.

Fourteen months later, on April 29, 1992, a jury in Sylmar, California—in the Simi Valley, where the trial had been moved to at the defendants' request—found one of the four officers charged in the case guilty of using excessive force. The other three were acquitted of all charges, and with that, the riot was on. By the time the violence ended, three days later, 50 people had died, more than 4,000 had been injured, 12,000 people had been arrested, and Los Angeles had sustained over $1 billion in property damages—a trail of destruction that nearly equaled the riots that swept through the Watts section of the city 26 years earlier.

This series of eyewitness accounts from staff members of the *Los Angeles Times* captures the unfolding drama of the riot almost as if it were a blood-stained ballet: how the riot began in what seemed to many righteous anger, spread beyond any semblance of reason to raw mayhem, and doubled back to bizarre rumor as the flames were dying out. The sequence appears in David Colbert's superb collection of first-person accounts, *Eyewitness to America*.

Dean E. Murphy

April 29, 3:45 p.m., the Simi Valley Courthouse. It was chaotic. Ten not-guilty verdicts had sent scores of reporters scrambling in every direction, searching for jurors, defendants, prosecutors, attorneys and community activists.

The jury and most of the defendants didn't want to talk. Sgt. Stacey C. Koon was nearly tackled by a throng of reporters and cameramen as he tried to slip away unnoticed. "You're guilty! You're guilty!" protesters shouted at a tight-lipped Koon, as the advancing crowd crushed a photographer against a parked car.

Inside the courthouse, Officer Laurence M. Powell—accused of striking the most blows on Rodney G. King—stood grinning in a klieg-lit second-floor briefing room. "I am very happy, very happy," he declared.

In response to a question, Powell said he had nothing to say to those upset by the verdicts. "I don't think I have to respond to them," he said. "They have to respond to themselves and make their own decision. I don't think there is anything I can do to change their feelings."

Kirk McCoy

April 29. 3:45 p.m., First A.M.E. Church, Mid-City. The mood at the First A.M.E. Church was somber. One could still see the shock and disbelief on the faces of the church members and all who gathered to watch as the verdicts were read.

"Not guilty, not guilty, not guilty."

Then I saw the Rev. Cecil (Chip) Murray.

Pounding his fist into his left hand, he began to cry.

"They gave us nothing, nothing. Not even a bone, dear God, not even a bone."

Shaw Hubler

April 29, 6:40 p.m., Florence and Normandie Avenues. A half-mile from the corner of Florence and Normandie, you could see the helicopters, swarming. Then, closer in, there were clots of people running, and over the scanner, the sound of police and TV crews telling each other, "Get out of there. Now."

There was gridlock. People lined the sidewalk six deep, shouting, gossiping, shaking their fists. Some held cans of beer and soda, some struggled home with children in their arms. They wore shorts and sport shirts. They looked like they had lined up for a Fourth of July parade.

In traffic, drivers were beginning to panic, pulling out into the paths of oncoming cars to make a quick getaway. As each car approached the intersection, young kids—teen-agers—were loping out, taking a look at the people inside and then heaving chunks of concrete and brick at anyone who wasn't black.

They looked so young, too young for the way their faces contorted with rage. Their wrists seemed so thin, their chests so frail. The rocks would slam into car after car, and you could hear the shouts. "Yeah, m___ f___! Oh, yeah!"

Kirk McCoy

April 29, 9 p.m., Manchester and Slauson Avenues. A colleague, Mike Meadows, and I were crisscrossing streets, looking for looters, when we drove by a liquor store at Manchester and Slauson. Four guys were taking what they could and were just beginning to start a fire. I was on the sidewalk across from the store when I heard someone behind me yell "M___ f___, stop taking pictures."

I turned to see a man, standing about 15 feet away, holding a bottle of liquor and aiming a gun at me. He fired. I turned and ran down the street to where Meadows was waiting in the car with the engine running.

In one of the worst riots in modern American history, looters in Los Angeles flee with stolen shoes from a Payless store. The spring 1992 riots were touched off by the acquittal on nearly all charges of four white police officers accused in the videotaped beating of a black motorist, Rodney King. (AP/Wide World Photo)

The guy fired five or six more shots as I ran.

If he had been sober I don't think I would have made it.

David Ferrell

April 30, 11:45 a.m., Manchester and Vermont Avenues. As we walked, we encountered a shirtless black man and his son, about 7, viewing the rubble. The man, who declined to give his name, talked of having heard all about Watts when he was young. Now, he wanted to show his own son the horrors of lawlessness. "It's stupid," he said bitterly. "It's just stupid."

Josh Meyer

April 30, 4 p.m., Mid-Town Shopping Center. As a fire nearby raged out of control, several police cars and hook and ladder trucks careened by, not stopping. One woman zoomed up to the front of the building in a late model Seville, a wild look in her eyes and a grin on her face. She jumped out of her car without rolling up the windows, leaving her screaming infant unattended. Then, the well-dressed, professional-looking woman sprinted into the store for her share.

Lee Harris

April 30, 11 p.m., Crenshaw Boulevard near Slauson Avenue. Something remained orderly even during the riot. Someone had ripped the front end of a Versateller in the Crenshaw Town Center. A crowd of men, women and children gathered and formed a line and began helping themselves to the money. One person would grab a handful of money and move out of the way for the next person.

Simples and his employees—armed with rifles and semiautomatic guns—had guarded it successfully for two nights, but left when the National Guard arrived. His lament was as much about the Guard's failure as it was about black life in Los Angeles. "All it is is building up our hopes for something," he said. "Always building up our hopes for something, to let us down."

Michael Moreau

May 1, Evening, Simi Valley. I headed home to Simi Valley over strangely abandoned freeways. Pulling off the 118 onto 1st Street, I drove the rental car to the garage where my car was being worked on.

While waiting for my bill, a tanned bleached blonde in shorts and a halter top came in and announced: "They say buses of them are supposed to be coming into town tonight." "Buses of who?" the garage owner asked. "Colored people," she said. "They say they're coming up here to start a riot."

I don't know where she got her information, perhaps from the source who told my neighbor the night before that there was looting at the Target store. Coincidentally, the neighbor had just been to Target and hadn't seen a thing.

∽

A mob's a monster; heads enough, but no brains.
    —Benjamin Franklin, *Poor Richard's Almanac*

Riffraff or Resister?

Seen on a television screen, the makeup of a mob such as the one that swept through Los Angeles in 1992 seems easy to parse. Some of its members are the honestly aggrieved; many more are opportunists who take advantage of the disorder to satisfy personal ends and desires, whether it's looting, torching, or inflicting random violence. Inside a mob, though, the story is often far more complicated.

This excerpt from a chapter titled "What Turns Individuals into Mobs" is taken from Jules Archer's book *Riot!* (The National Advisory Commission on Civil Disorders is the so-called Kerner Commission, named for former Illinois Gov. Otto Kerner and formed to investigate the mass civil disturbances of the 1960s.)

Americans have generally assumed that those who make up rioting mobs represent only a tiny fraction of their racial, religious, political, or economic groups. Conspicuous are a riffraff fringe of ne'er-do-wells, juvenile delinquents, idlers, troublemakers, and criminal types. President [Lyndon] Johnson attributed the ghetto uprisings of the 1960s to a few "mean and willful men."

Gov. George Wallace of Alabama charged that riots of the decade were the work of a small conspiracy of Communist agitators bent upon destroying American society.

The "riffraff" theory is popular because it reassures the majority of Americans that there is no serious flaw in their society, since the rioting reflects only the dissatisfaction of a tiny minority. If only riffraff are involved, then all that is necessary to prevent future riots is to muzzle them forcefully and ban outside agitators. That eliminates any need to face serious social problems that may be at the bottom of the disturbances and that would take painful change and readjustment by the majority to correct.

But the National Advisory Commission on Civil Disorders found "no evidence that all or any of the disorders ... were planned or directed by any organization or group, international, national, or local." It found further that the typical rioter was *not* a member of the criminal, unemployed, or migrant "underclass."

May 4, 1970: Antiwar demonstrators at Kent State University scatter as the National Guard fires tear gas into their midst. Later, four students would be killed and nine wounded when guardsmen, egged on by students throwing stones, opened fire on the crowd. (© Reuters NewMedia Inc./CORBIS)

Like the tip of an iceberg, the mob often reflects a much larger mass resistance hidden from view. The Governor's Commission on the Los Angeles Riots reported in 1966 that while most blacks in the city did not themselves participate in the Watts riots, most nevertheless supported the rioters.

The Beast Within

Given a forceful enough stimulus, mob behavior can sometimes seem justified, at least in its early stages. But when even the semblance of a reason drops out of rioting, we're left with the naked violence itself. Without pretext to fall back on, the animalistic behavior of the participants and the capacity of crowd psychology to obliterate all moral sense stand out in stark relief.

Driven to the edge, or so they think, investors go on rampages, just as soccer fans do. Most of the time the moment passes quickly, and we're left with little more than a damaged industry sector or section of a stadium in shambles. But when the beast within the crowd gets out, far worse things can happen. So it was in the notorious 1989 attack on a jogger in New York's Central Park—an event that came to epitomize an urban phenomenon known quite accurately as "wilding."

In this account from the May 8, 1989, issue of *Newsweek* magazine by reporter David Gelman with Peter McKillop, a number of experts offer up reasons why the "wilders" behaved as they did, but what we're left with, more than motivation, is the sheer senselessness of it all. The woman the group attacked, raped, and nearly killed recovered from her injuries and eventually participated in and completed the New York City Marathon.

On a warm April night two weeks ago a band of young black and Hispanic teenagers chased down a young Wall Street investment banker out jogging by herself, rather daringly for that late hour, in Central Park. They hit the slightly built woman with fists and rocks, stabbed her head five times and then repeatedly raped and sodomized her. When she was found hours later she had suffered multiple skull fractures and lost most of her blood. Last week she remained in a coma, with indications of serious brain damage.

By early accounts, the seven youths charged with the attack were hardly casebook sociopaths. They were variously vouched for by friends, teachers and relatives as industrious, churchgoing, "shy." Individually there seemed nothing especially intimidating about them. Yet together they stood accused of an assault so wantonly vicious that, as an investigator for the Manhattan district attorney's office remarked, "even New York" was unprepared for its brutality.

151

Indeed, besides their shock at the savagery of the attack, New Yorkers were scarcely ready for yet another explosion of the white-black tensions that have wracked the city in recent years. Many, white and nonwhite alike, hastened to say the incident had more to do with class than race—a lashing out of resentful ghetto residents against privileged Yuppies. In that view, they were supported by at least one black psychiatrist, James Comer of the Yale Child Study Center, for whom the episode seemed "as much an issue of the haves and have-nots as it is race." But to Comer and others, there appeared also to be forces at work—part adolescent restlessness, part "herd" mentality—having little to do with either race or class.

Originally, police say, about 35 youths, some as young as 13, had gone into the park "wilding"—a variety of bash-as-bash-can gang ram-page that has disrupted some of the city's public places recently. After a couple of desultory attempts on a male jogger and a homeless man, the group dwindled to a hard core of about eight to 13. Ultimately, seven are believed to have participated in the rape of the woman jog-ger. Such expeditions usually begin spontaneously. Teenagers hanging around a housing project often have no agenda but to stir up a little excitement. "They may have said, 'Let's go wilding,'" notes Franklin Zimring, director of the Earl Warren Legal Institute at the University of California, "but nobody said, 'Let's go raping.'" Zimring, who con-ducted a 1984 study of youth homicide in New York, thinks the group may have been swayed by what he calls "government by dare—you do it because you don't want to back out."

Behavioral experts agree that in the dynamics of a group, there is often at least one leader able to control the rest by playing on their need to prove themselves. The instigator of a gang rape gains a dou-ble sense of mastery, not only over the victim but over his cohorts, who feel obliged to equal his audacity. There is an undeniably subtle power in the group: It has the ability to validate and thereby embolden behavior. That may be especially true of teenagers, who are particularly susceptible to pressure from peers. But the essential element is the anonymity group membership confers, and thus the relative freedom from accountability. "Basically, it's a loss of the indi-vidual's personality," says Robert Panzarella, a professor of police sci-ence at New York's John Jay College of Criminal Justice. "Things he would never think of doing by himself he does in the group." There is also a kind of division of labor, with the chilling result that "while the action of each individual can seem relatively minor, the action of the whole may be horrific."

Something like that process was evident in the Central Park rape. As the defendants themselves told it later, it was one of the group, a 15-year-old, who first spotted the woman and said, "Go get her." Another, 14, helped knock her down, then punched and kicked her. Others, in turn, hit her with a rock, a brick and a length of lead pipe, pinioned her legs and arms, ripped off her shirt and sweat pants, and committed the actual rape and sodomy. "No one really knows these kids or what was in their minds," cautions Yale's Comer. But by their own description there appears to have been an accelerating frenzy that is often seen in gang rapes. Momentum builds as the assailants try to outdo one another, in this case a momentum that carried them over the edge into horror.

Although newspapers reported when the youths were arraigned that they appeared to show no "remorse," some observers doubt that they have yet grasped the enormity of their collective act. On the other hand, Dorothy Lewis, a criminal psychiatrist known for her work with serial killer Ted Bundy, warns that initial newspaper reports stressing the apparent wholesomeness of some of the group should be viewed with a measure of skepticism. Lewis believes further investigation will show that the teenagers who committed the rape were damaged in some way. In similar cases, she says, people who commit such acts have either been victims of abuse themselves or have witnessed terrible scenes of domestic violence. These early experiences make the youths "unable to control their impulses," and, in essence, she thinks that is what could have happened that night in Central Park. "I see something," says Lewis, "that started out as a roaming gang, but degenerated into a heinous, aberrant crime."

∾

There was not that variety of beasts in the ark, as is of beastly natures in the multitude.

—Ben Jonson, *Explorata*

On August 7, 1930, a mob in Marion, Indiana, raided the county jail and carried away three black teenagers accused of murdering a young white man and raping his girlfriend. Two of the teenagers, Thomas Shipp and Abram Smith, were lynched, their hanging bodies kept on display for days afterwards as a warning to other African Americans. No one in Marion was ever convicted of the murders. (© Bettmann/CORBIS)

Lynching: Thinking About
the Unthinkable

Like rioting, lynching seems to rest, in the minds of its participants, on a rationale: The law is insufficient to the task; defenseless womanhood isn't safe on the streets; the murder of one black or Jew or Chinese or [fill in the blank] is necessary to teach all blacks, Jews, Chinese, or what have you a lesson. Like wilding, lynching also strips away any veneer of civilization, any hint of the progress of the species.

The entries that follow, along with the accompanying photographs and political cartoon, represent an effort to capture these acts of mob "justice" in all their horrifying complexity: from the point of view of someone who witnessed one at a far too young age, through poetry and song, through an analysis of motive, and via Mark Twain, as a searing study of the psychology of crowds. In the first of the entries, part of a 1985 interview by Charles Hardy III for National Public Radio's *Horizons* show, an elderly black man recalled a lynching he had witnessed 83 years earlier, as a five year old in his hometown of Jacksonville, Florida.

"They Burned a Negro Right at the Stake There"

They had a big cross. The Ku Klux Klan, they burned a Negro right at the stake there. And oh, it was a terrible thing. You could smell his burning flesh five miles and it was a terrible thing. And do you know, those Ku Klux Klan after the flames were over, and he was burnt to a crisp, go around and cut things off of him—off of the fingers and toes—and give to these white women. And they'd take 'em home, the white women with their children, take 'em home, and put 'em in glass jars and set 'em on the mantle piece. "And those? Well this is what we do to niggers. See that nigger's toes, this nigger's uh, uh, uh?"

You see those are the things that made me know that they ever put their hand on me, I would kill 'em just as long as I could. Because I know what they would do. They'll punish me, and make me suffer. But I know if I started to killin' 'em, they'd kill me just like that and I'd be gone.

Billie Holiday's "Strange Fruit Hanging from the Poplar Trees"

As one of the most profound and shocking expressions of mankind's inhumanity to itself, lynching has long attracted the interest of writers and poets. This blues lyric was written by a New York City schoolteacher named Abel Meeropol, who used the pseudonym Lewis Allen, and first performed by Billie Holiday in 1939, under the title "Strange Fruit."

> Southern trees bear a strange fruit
> Blood on the leaves and blood at the root
> Black boy swingin' in the Southern breeze
> Strange fruit hanging from the poplar trees
>
> Pastoral scene of the gallant South
> The bulging eyes and the twisted mouth
> Scent of magnolia sweet and fresh
> And the sudden smell of burning flesh
>
> Here is a fruit for the crows to pluck
> For the rain to gather, for the wind to suck
> For the sun to rot, for the tree to drop
> Here is a strange and bitter crop.

I believe mobs are all possessed of a thousand demons. They are the people of psychological epidemics of historical mass convulsions.

—Sigmund Freud

Leo Frank hanging from a tree in Frey's Mill, Georgia, on the morning of August 17, 1915. Accused of murdering one of his employees, the Cornell-educated Frank had been abducted from a Georgia state prison by a vigilante group.

An Outcome
"Altogether Predictable"

Scapegoats come in all shapes and sizes. Individual companies can be scapegoats, their sales or stock price made to pay for the sins of an industry sector. In the wake of the collapse of the Internet bubble market, investors went looking for analysts to blame for decisions that ultimately had been driven by the investors' own greed and irrational exuberance. Politicians and CEOs become scapegoats, too, forced to do penance for economic and geopolitical conditions far beyond their powers to influence. So, of course, do ethnic and racial minorities. Finding an outsider, an "other," to blame makes a crowd feel less culpable for its own individual and collective shortcomings even when the blame is carried to horrible extremes.

In 1913, Leo Frank, a New York Jew who had moved to Atlanta to manage a pencil factory, was found guilty of the murder of one of his employees, 14-year-old Mary Phagan. Sentenced to death by hanging, largely on the shaky testimony of a janitor who himself had been suspected in the crime, Frank had his sentence commuted to life in prison by the Georgia governor. Because of the nature of the crime and the controversial commutation, the case attracted broad attention throughout the country and especially in Georgia, where public outrage was fanned by the demagogic U.S. senator and publisher Tom Watson.

Two years later, in August 1915, 25 armed men calling themselves the Knights of Mary Phagan cut the telephone lines to the Georgia State Prison at Milledgeville, where Frank was being held, entered the prison, and made off with Frank into the night. Sometime the next morning, near Mary Phagan's childhood home, the raiding party put a noose around Leo Frank's neck and hanged him. In the following excerpt, University of Florida historian W. Fitzhugh Brundage examines the rationale behind one of the most infamous nonblack lynchings in American history.

Little about the lynching of Leo Frank, on August 17, 1915, was commonplace. Frank's ethnicity, notoriety, and class set him apart from most victims of mobs during the heyday of lynching in the United States (1880–1940). Probably fewer than 350 whites, as compared to perhaps as many as four thousand blacks, died at the hands of Southern mobs during that era. But if Frank's lynching deviates from the routine patterns of lynching, it nevertheless reveals much about the culture that sustained the phenomenon well into this century and could claim the life of so unlikely a victim as Leo Frank.

During the late nineteenth century, lynchers, especially in the frontier West, had claimed a steady toll of white victims. Ethnic minorities—Mexicans, Italians, and Chinese—sometimes fell prey to vigilantes in both the South and the West. But by the second decade of the twentieth century, lynching had become primarily a Southern and a racial phenomenon. By then, the lynching of whites had become a rarity—over ninety-five percent of mob victims were African-American. So how then can we explain the summary execution of Frank?

Frank, like most white lynching victims in the South, was a conspicuous outsider. Mob violence against whites drew heavily upon xenophobia, bigotry, and white Southerners' strong, indeed almost instinctual, urge to distinguish between full members of the community and interlopers. Frank, of course, was doubly reviled as both a Northern-born Jew and an industrialist. As a Jew, he was the target of ferocious anti-Semitic attacks which exploited Southern whites' suspicion of immigrants and non-Protestants. And as a Northern industrialist, he was easily caricatured as a capitalist exploiter of impoverished and vulnerable Southern whites, especially young mill women like his alleged victim, Mary Phagan.

In addition to his status as an outsider and a member of a persecuted faith, Frank was charged with the crime most likely to provoke white Southerners to condone summary justice. While even trivial transgressions by blacks might inflame whites, murders and assaults by whites often were accepted in a matter-of-fact way by other Southern whites. Neither a heinous crime nor an unsavory reputation was usually adequate to incite extralegal violence against an offending white. The combination of the two, however, could stir communal vengeance. The affront allegedly committed by Frank— the rape and murder of a virginal white girl—was the same charge that provoked the majority of lynchings of whites in the South. Thus,

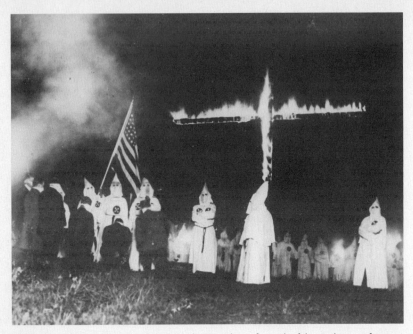

The Klu Klux Klan was founded in 1867, in the immediate aftermath of the Civil War. Fifty-seven years later, in 1924, Klansmen gathered on the Virginia shore of the Potomac River to celebrate the hate-group's anniversary. This burning cross was visible from the White House.

so great was the dishonor attached to both Frank's alleged offense and his ethnicity that many Southern whites concluded that he deserved to suffer the fate that they otherwise reserved for African-Americans.

Class tensions comprised the final catalyst for Frank's death. The nationwide campaign to defend Frank offended many Georgians, and the commutation of his sentence seemed to confirm Tom Watson's warnings that chicanery would shelter Frank from justice while the honor of a common Southern mill woman, or, in Watson's endearing phrase, "a daughter of the people," went undefended. Long before Frank's lynching, leading Southern lawyers argued that mobs resorted to summary justice because of a legitimate fear that well-paid lawyers used due process of law to hamper the punishment of criminals (especially well-heeled criminals). Discontent focused on the complexities of the law and trial procedures. The governors' pardoning powers were no less suspect than the fairness of the courts. A governor's respite or pardon of a condemned criminal, as in Frank's case, sometimes stiffed communities to substitute their punishment for the less certain punishment of the state. Sensationalized reporting of Frank's trial, of the campaign to defend him, and of Governor Slaton's decision to commute his sentence, fed all of these long-simmering fears about shyster lawyers, tardy justice, and corrupt politicians who were susceptible to outside influence.

However threadbare, these rationales for lynching contributed to the respectability of mob violence and enabled many Southern whites to exonerate and justify Frank's murder as the only remedy available to a provoked populace. For all these reasons, Frank's murder at the hands of a mob, however shocking, was altogether predictable.

Mark Twain: "The Pitifulest Thing Out Is a Mob"

The collapse of Enron and the subsequent parade of its top executives to Capitol Hill provided a valuable lesson in the modern approach to dealing with the metaphorical lynch mob of a congressional subcommittee: spin, obfuscate, look suitably contrite where appropriate, and when all else fails plead the Fifth Amendment. Nearly 125 years earlier, Mark Twain offered up another, better model of how to face down a strutting, angry crowd.

No moment in American literature does a better job of capturing the mind of a lynch mob than this one, from Twain's *The Adventures of Huckleberry Finn*. In less than two pages, Twain shows the mob first in full flush, then in full flight. The scene is made more complicated by the justifiable anger of the crowd: Colonel Sherburn, the object of its wrath, has just murdered in broad daylight a drunken local who had been cursing him on the streets of the dusty Arkansas river town where the action occurs. In Sherburn, though, the lynch mob has more than met its match.

They swarmed up the street towards Sherburn's house, a-whooping and yelling and raging like Injuns, and everything had to clear the way or get run over and tromped to mush, and it was awful to see. Children was heeling it ahead of the mob, screaming and trying to get out of the way, and every window along the road was full of women's heads, and there was nigger boys in every tree, and bucks and wenches looking over every fence; and as soon as the mob would get nearly to them they would break and skedaddle back out of reach. Lots of the women and girls was crying and taking on, scared most to death.

They swarmed up in front of Sherburn's palings as thick as they could jam together, and you couldn't hear yourself think for the noise. It was a little twenty-foot yard. Some sung out, "Tear down the fence! Tear down the fence!" Then there was a racket of ripping and tearing and smashing, and down she goes, and the front wall of the crowd begins to roll in like a wave.

On April 25, 1959, Charles Parker was abducted from a Mississippi prison where he was awaiting trial on charges of raping a white woman. Parker's dead body was recovered from a river nine days later. He had been shot twice. Herblock drew this depiction of Parker's abduction for the *Washington Post*. [Poplarville, Mississippi, U.S.A., 1959—from Straight Herblock (Simon & Schuster, 1964)]

Just then Sherburn steps out on to the roof of his little front porch, with a double-barrel gun in his hand, and takes his stand, perfectly ca'm and deliberate, not saying a word. The racket stopped and the wave sucked back.

Sherburn never said a word—just stood there, looking down. The stillness was awful creepy and uncomfortable. Sherburn run his eye slow along the crowd; and wherever it struck, the people tried a little to outgaze him, but they couldn't; they dropped their eyes and looked sneaky. Then pretty soon Sherburn sort of laughed; not the pleasant kind, but the kind that makes you feel like when you are eating bread that's got sand in it.

Then he says, slow and scornful:

"The idea of you lynching anybody! It's amusing. The idea of you thinking you had pluck enough to lynch a *man!* Because you're brave enough to tar and feather poor friendless cast-out women that come along here, did that make you think you had grit enough to lay your hands on a *man?* Why, a *man's* safe in the hands of ten thousand of your kind—as long as it's day-time and you're not behind him.

"Do I know you? I know you clear through. I was born and raised in the South, and I've lived in the North; so I know the average all around. The average man's a coward. In the North he lets anybody walk over him that wants to, and goes home and prays for a humble spirit to bear it. In the South one man, all by himself, has stopped a stage full of men, in the day-time, and robbed the lot. Your newspapers call you a brave people so much that you think you *are* braver than any other people—whereas you're just *as* brave, and no braver. Why don't your juries hang murderers? Because they're afraid the man's friends will shoot them in the back, in the dark—and it's just what they *would* do.

"So they always acquit; and then a *man* goes in the night, with a hundred masked cowards at his back, and lynches the rascal. Your mistake is that you didn't bring a man with you, that's one mistake, and the other is that you didn't come in the dark and fetch your masks. You brought *part* of a man—Buck Harkness, there—and if you hadn't had him to start you, you'd a taken it out in blowing.

"You didn't want to come. The average man don't like trouble and danger. *You* don't like trouble and danger. But if only *half* a man—like Buck Harkness, there—shouts 'Lynch him, lynch him!' you're afraid to back down—afraid you'll be found out to be what you are—cowards—and so you raise a yell, and hang yourselves onto that half-a-man's coat tail, and come raging up here, swearing what big things you're going to do. The pitifulest thing out is a mob; that's what an army is—a mob; they don't fight with courage that's born in them, but with courage that's borrowed from their mass, and from their officers. But a mob without any *man* at the head of it is *beneath* pitifulness. Now the thing for *you* to do, is to droop your tails and go home and crawl in a hole. If any real lynching's going to be done it will be done in the dark, Southern fashion; and when they come they'll bring their masks, and fetch a *man* along. Now *leave*—and take your half-a-man with you"—tossing his gun up across his left arm and cocking it, when he says this.

The crowd washed back sudden, and then broke all apart and went tearing off every which way, and Buck Harkness he heeled it after them, looking tolerable cheap. I could a staid, if I'd a wanted to, but I didn't want to.

Lawmen gathered at the University of Mississippi in September 1962 prepare to confront integrationists. (Charles Moore/Stockphoto)

The mentality of the frenzied crowd isn't limited to protestors and outsiders. Authorities also can take on the worst characteristics of a mob. In this famous photo by Bill Hudson of the Associated Press, Birmingham, Alabama, police turn their dogs loose on a protester during a 1963 demonstration led by the Southern Christian Leadership Conference. (AP/Wide World Photo)

～

A terrible thing is a mob when it has villains to lead it.
—Euripides

"The Men Snarled and Shouted As They Flung Their Stones"

This description of a public stoning, the ancient predecessor to lynching, provides a modern example of a crowd administering justice. This time, though, the mob is acting at the behest of the state. The dispatch, by reporter R.M. Macoll, appeared in the February 11, 1958, London *Daily Express*. The dateline is Jeddah, the second-largest city of Saudi Arabia.

The unending procession of brand new giant American cars nosed slowly along the dusty street.

The shop windows nearby were crammed with glittering goods—refrigerators and air-conditioners from America, cameras from Germany, electrical fittings from Italy.

Round the corner plasterers were hard at work putting the finishing touches to a twelve-story modernistic office building, one of scores that are being rushed to a finish all over the bursting, bustling seaport of Jeddah.

But the big and silent crowd had eyes for none of this.

A prince, a nephew of the king, sat stern-faced on a chair. Before him was a strip of carpet. From a lorry a man was led forward by two khaki-clad policemen. He was in his late twenties and was completely composed.

His hands were chained together behind him and he walked awkwardly because of the chains festooned about his ankles.

Arrived at the edge of the carpet, he knelt and was told by the police to keep his eyes fixed on the prince's face.

At his side an official unrolled a scroll and started to read aloud the man's misdeeds and the punishment decreed by the court. The crowd was now utterly hushed.

Suddenly the line of police parted and the executioner appeared, sword in hand. He approached the victim from behind and on tiptoe. As the reading stopped the executioner bent and touched the kneeling man lightly on the back with his finger.

Instinctively the man started, and in so doing raised his head. On the instant, with a swift and expert blow, the executioner decapitated him.

A long, slow sigh came from the onlookers.

Now a woman was dragged forward. She and the man had together murdered her former husband. She, too, was under thirty, and slender.

The recital of her crime too was read out as she knelt and then the executioner stepped forward with a wooden stave and dealt a hundred blows with all his strength upon her shoulder.

As the flogging ended the woman sagged over on her side.

Next, a lorry loaded with rocks and stones was backed up and its cargo deposited in a pile. At a signal from the prince the crowd leaped on the stones and started pelting the woman to death.

It was difficult to determine how she was facing her last and awful ordeal, since she was veiled in Muslim fashion and her mouth was gagged to muffle her cries.

Had this scene been taking place in the middle of the desert it would have been grim enough; but that it should have been enacted in the heart of modern Jeddah's business neighborhood lent it a dismally macabre quality.

The sun shone down from a glorious blue sky. A familiar American soft-drink advertisement showed its gentle blandishments. "Come to the Middle East," pleaded an airlines travel poster in a nearby window. "Savour its romance, its colour, its quaint traditions. . . ."

The crowd were no longer silent. The men snarled and shouted as they flung their stones, their faces transformed into masks of sadism.

The execution of the man? Well, let us not forget that it was as recently as 1936 that the French held their last public execution. And the beheading was at least humanely and quickly carried out.

But the doing to death of the woman is something which the handful of horrified Europeans in the crowd will not quickly forget.

It took just over an hour before the doctor in attendance, who halted the stoning periodically to feel the victim's pulse, announced her dead.

This double execution took place just the other day.

∿

A mob ... is as difficult to follow to its various sources as the sea itself; nor does the parallel stop here. For the ocean is not more fickle and uncertain, more terrible when roused, more unreasonable or cruel.

—Charles Dickens

On May 10, 1849, some 15,000 people gathered at New York City's Astor Place Opera House to protest the appearance of an English Shakespearean actor who had done little to hide his contempt for his audiences. When the crowd wouldn't disperse, militia opened fire, killing 23 protesters, more than twice as many Americans as died in the Battle of New Orleans. This lithograph of the riot is by Currier & Ives.

Rwanda:
When the Mob Is the State,
Horror Becomes Ordinary

A mob in a frenzy is always dangerous, whether it's acting economically or politically or simply seeking revenge. But when the mob and state become one and the same, the potential for horror is the greatest of all. In the small African nation of Rwanda in 1994, all the elements were in place for a harrowing example of genocide at work.

Rwandans had historically been divided into two ethnic groups: the majority Hutus, about 90 percent of the population, and the minority Tutsis. Between the end of World War I and the country's first democratic election in 1959, Tutsis ruled for the most part, installed in place by Belgian masters in a divide-and-conquer policy widely practiced in colonial Africa. Violence followed the 1959 vote that brought the majority Hutus to power. Old rifts deepened in the decades ahead, and by the early 1990s, demagogues were pouring gasoline on the fire.

Agathe Habyarimana, the wife of the president, established a newspaper called *Kangura—Wake It Up!*—that advocated "Hutu Power" through the "Hutu Ten Commandments," including Commandment Eight: "Hutus must stop having mercy on Tutsis." Supported by the government, young Hutu males began organizing themselves into militias known as *Interahamwe.* Not to be outdone, the country's vice-president in a November 1992 speech called for Hutus to force all Tutsis to leave Rwanda. If they didn't, it was up to the Hutu people to "destroy" the "cockroaches."

A year and a half later, the violence began in earnest. By the time it ended, 800,000 of Rwanda's seven million inhabitants, most of them Tutsis, were dead, two million people had fled the country, and another two million had been forced to leave their homes and villages.

In this excerpt from a lengthy investigation by Human Rights Watch, one is struck by the seeming ordinariness of such extraordinary and horrifying events—what Hannah Arendt once called "the banality of evil." Butare, the scene of the action, lies well southwest of the Rwandan capital of Kigali, near the border with Burundi. At the time the slaughter began, in April 1994, Butare was the center of a subdistrict of about 26,000 people, about a quarter of them Tutsis.

As in Kigali, soldiers . . . along with National Police began the slaughter by targeting people from the intellectual and political elite of Butare. They went directly to the homes of those selected ahead of time for slaughter, sometimes relying on local guides or asking directions from neighbors. Militia backed up the members of the regular armed forces. In addition to the dozens of Interahamwe who had apparently been discreetly brought in during the previous ten days, one hundred or so Presidential Guards and militia arrived in Butare on April 20.

A C-130 transport plane landed at Butare airport between 4 and 5 p.m., perhaps the first time such a large craft had used the small landing strip. Struck by the arrival of such an unusual plane and by the appearance of unknown soldiers and militia in town that evening, many people assumed that the strangers had been flown into Butare. In fact, they had arrived by bus while the plane, flown by Belgian pilots, had come from Nairobi to evacuate a group of European nuns and U.N. military observers. In addition to militia from outside Butare, local killers reportedly led by Shalom Ntahobari also began the most damaging of their attacks on April 20.

Although soldiers and militia killed some people in their homes, they took many to be executed at one or another of the main killing grounds, like that behind the museum or in the arboretum of the university or near the psychiatric center and the Groupe Scolaire. Beginning late in the day of April 20 and continuing for the next three days, residents of Butare town reported hearing frequent bursts of gunfire, particularly from these execution grounds.

The soldiers began the slaughter in the pleasant neighborhood of Buye, striking leading Tutsis like Professor Karenzi. Presidential Guards from the group that protected [Rwandan president Jean-Baptiste] Habyarimana's brother, Dr. Bararengana, came for Karenzi at about 2 p.m. on April 21 and took him to the barrier manned by soldiers of the ESO in front of the Hotel Faucon. There he was lined up with a number of other people, including another professor who was accused of having falsified his identity card. According to a witness, a militia member from out of town then killed two men, two women, and five children under the eyes of Prefect Nsabimana and Vice-Rector Nshimyumuremyi, who stood a short distance down the street, in front of the Hotel Ibis. One of the other men bolted and ran for his life, and Professor Karenzi was shot and killed immediately afterwards. Soldiers returned shortly after to the Karenzi home and murdered the professor's wife. The children and young people of the household were hidden in the ceiling and escaped, although all except one would later be killed, too. . . .

In addition to political and intellectual leaders, the military targeted the rich. In the heart of Butare, soldiers invaded the home of a prosperous businessman on April 20 and extorted some 300,000 Rwandan francs (about U.S. $1,700) as the price of his own life and that of his family. Two days later, a young soldier named Claude came back with three Interahamwe, reportedly from the group headed by Shalom. They took five young adults and a twelve-year-old boy with them and walked the short distance to the killing field at the Groupe Scolaire where they murdered them. In Tumba six National Policemen led a crowd in attacking the home of a Swiss entrepreneur who had a Tutsi wife. The ordinary people were armed with machetes, spears, and even a bow and arrow—wielded by a young man wearing a baseball cap with the visor behind, in the fashion of foreign young people. The National Policemen fired a couple of warning shots and forced their way in. After having robbed the family of several hundred thousand Rwandan francs, they called in the civilians, who looted the house. Some of the crowd stole valuable items, but others seemed almost embarrassed at what they were doing and took items of little or no value, like a cooking pot full of potatoes or a child's toy. To one observer, they seemed to be participating because they had no choice. They left without injuring anyone.

Soldiers killed important Hutu who were thought to oppose the genocide, just as other troops had killed Hutu officials of the national government in Kigali. According to witnesses, Nizeyimana and soldiers of his guard murdered his neighbor, Deputy Prosecutor Matabaro. Soldiers also slew the professor Jean-Marie Vianney Maniraho, who had criticized the heavy military presence in town at a public security meeting, and his family. In Cyarwa, soldiers burned down the home of a Hutu woman related to a national leader of the MDR who opposed Hutu Power. Several days later, she was killed at a barrier, reportedly on the order of Deputy Baravuga. Soldiers and militia killed the sub-prefect Zéphanie Nyilinkwaya and fourteen others of his family during the night of April 21. A Hutu member of the PSD, Nyilinkwaya was seen as a potential leader of resistance to the slaughter of Tutsi. A MSF doctor came by Nyilinkwaya's house early on the morning of April 22 and found the corpses of the family scattered over the drive in front of the house. Among them was a child three months old, shot in the back of the head, lying at his mother's breast, which had also been blown open by a bullet. The doctor found two survivors, a girl about seventeen years old, who had been shot by a bullet that had passed through both breasts, and a fourteen-year-old boy. When he prepared to take them to the hospital, two soldiers came at the run to stop him. It was only by insistent negotiating that the doctor won the right to take the wounded for treatment.

∾

Thousands of isolated individuals may acquire at certain moments, and under the influence of certain violent emotions—such, for example, as a great national event—the characteristics of a psychological crowd.
— Gustave Le Bon, *The Crowd*

Boston, April 1976: Ted Landsmark, an African American and executive director of the Boston Contractors Association, was on his way to a meeting at City Hall when antibusing demonstrators assailed him, using the flag as a makeshift weapon. This haunting photo of the attack was taken by Stanley J. Forman of the *Boston Herald*. (Stanley J. Forman/Boston Herald)

Keeping Your Head When All About You Are Losing Theirs

Think of a lynching as a murder-by-mob, and it's almost impossible to project yourself into the scene, either as one of those who does the roping or even as a witness to the grisly spectacle. Yet, of course, the annals are filled with accounts of vigilante hangings in the South and Old West that drew large and often enthusiastic crowds.

If lynchings are hard to make an imaginative connection with, genocide is all the harder. Who could turn the other way as neighbors and fellow countrymen are murdered wholesale because of their ethnicity or religion or tribal affiliation? Worse still, who could begin to take part? History, though, harbors far too many examples of respectable people who did just that. How can it be?

On another level, how is it that a demonstration that sets out early in the day with such lofty goals—to save the environment, to assure civil or human rights, to protest injustice—can end in violent confrontation with police officers or National Guardsmen who might be our neighbors' children?

The explanation, I believe, is that we resist thinking of crowd violence, lynchings, and even genocides as what they really are: extreme forms of the emotional justice that we administer all the time. We punish our children too often based less on what they've done than on how we feel at the moment we are confronted with what they have done—exhausted from the work day or angry from a dressing down by our boss that the 10 year old in front of us had nothing to do with.

We punish stocks, too, for thoroughly emotional reasons: not because their intrinsic worth has collapsed but because they have fallen out of favor. The Internet bubble market was filled with examples—solid, laudable companies that investors wouldn't touch, and little more than shell companies that the same investors couldn't leave alone.

So it is, too, with the greater issues we've been considering in this section. Faced with a line of guardsmen who won't yield to our demands, we give way to our frustration and begin hurling rocks; and the guardsmen give way to their own emotions, respond in far greater kind, and the melee is on. Absent evidence that would stand up in any court of law, we take justice into our own hand. Goaded by authorities and afraid of bucking the majority, we project our own insecurities—our past failures and fears for the future—onto some "other," and the massacre is on.

Emotional justice seeks scapegoats, the modern incarnation of those literal goats who were bedecked with representations of a community's miseries and then kicked out of the herd or slaughtered. Our human nature drives us to it, and the mass media edges the process along by showing us the grieving family who claims that justice wasn't done. Real justice, though, asks for more. Real justice demands evidence that stands up in the court of the intellect, not the court of the emotions.

As with so much else in this book, the vital issue is to do due diligence not only on the proposition in front of you but on your own motivations for resisting or acceding to it. Is it reason that's driving you, or emotion? Have you examined the logic of the charges, or are you swept up in the emotion that surrounds them?

It's also critical to realize that once mob rule gets loose, once the normal laws of civility are laid aside, the crowd can slue in any direction. In his "Declaration of Guilt" delivered in 1945, the Protestant theologian Martin Neimoller said famously: "In Germany they came first for the Communists, and I didn't speak up because I wasn't a Communist. Then they came for the Jews, and I didn't speak up because I wasn't a Jew. Then they came for the trade unionists, and I didn't speak up because I wasn't a trade unionist. Then they came for Catholics, and I didn't speak up because I was a Protestant. Then they came for me, and by that time no one was left to speak up." Make that sort of empathetic leap *before*, not *after* the mob does its work, and it becomes almost impossible to go along with the madness of the crowd.

Not long after the start of World War II, eight Nazi agents slipped ashore on the East Coast of the United States, armed with explosives to destroy bridges, aluminum plants, power plants, and other targets. When the tiny invasion force was captured, President Franklin Roosevelt ordered that its members be tried in a secret military tribunal. The task of defending the saboteurs was assigned to a North Carolina lawyer and veteran of World War I, Kenneth Royall. There the matter might have ended, below the radar of history, had Royall gone along with the plan, but secret tribunals struck him as another example of the extremes of emotional justice.

German agents or not, saboteurs or not, Royall felt that his clients deserved the full protections of a civil trial, and he argued thus up to the U.S. Supreme Court.

Although the Court finally agreed to one of his key points, Royall lost the case. His clients were convicted in secret, and six of the eight were executed before their attorney even knew the sentence had been imposed. He lost the case, too, in the court of public opinion. His home-state *Charlotte Observer* pilloried Royall as a "braying ass" for bucking the emotional tide of the moment and standing for his own deep-seated principles. Other newspaper and public commentators were no less unkind. Ultimately, though, the principles, not the emotion, prevailed. Far from being disgraced, Royall was promoted to brigadier general and later to undersecretary of war. In 1947, Roosevelt's successor, Harry Truman, made him what proved to be the nation's last secretary of war.

Kenneth Royall knew that in times of crisis, emotions are our most unsteady guide—the rawer they are, the less likely they are to lead us true. Like Martin Neimoller, Royall knew, too, that the same court that could try his clients in secret might someday want to try him that way, too.

~

So when at times the mob is swayed
To carry praise or blame too far,
We may take something like a star
To stay our minds on and be staid.
—Robert Frost, "Take Something Like A Star"

5

LEADERS & FOLLOWERS

Introduction

"Whoso would be a man must first be a nonconformist," Ralph Waldo Emerson wrote in his essay "Self-Reliance." Later in the essay, Emerson came back to the point and broadened the message: "It is easy in the world to live after the world's opinion; it is easy in solitude to live after our own; but the great man is he who in the midst of the crowd keeps with perfect sweetness the independence of solitude."

Generations of American individualists have taken heart from these words. To wartime pacifists, Emerson issued a call to stand their ground, despite a torrent of public sentiment flowing in the opposite direction. To the hippies and beatniks of the counterculture, he granted a license to snub their noses at convention, holding that "a foolish consistency is the hobgoblin of little minds." The fact, though, is that human beings like to go in the other direction. We're communal beasts for the most part. Just as packs of wolves look for alpha males to lead them, so we look for alpha humans to direct us on the way.

Marketers often try to take advantage of our follow-the-leader instincts by aiming new products not at the broad middle of the market they hope eventually to reach, but at the razor-thin start of the market: the early adopters who set the trends that the rest of us follow. A new line of teenage clothing might first be marketed aggressively in the inner city, where total sales ultimately will be relatively few. But what gets worn on the mean streets has a chance of finding its way up onto the backs of rappers; rap acts end up on MTV; and such is the power of mass communication that the tastes of ghetto teens determine the consumption desires of suburban and exurban kids who wouldn't walk through Harlem or Watts or Cabrini-Green on a bet.

Along with other London investors, Nathan Rothschild of the famous banking dynasty watched the 1815 Battle of Waterloo with rapt attention. If Napoleon defeated the British and Prussian forces, the price of British bonds was sure to collapse. If the English triumphed, the reverse would happen. But unlike other investors, Rothschild had an edge: an intelligence system based on carrier pigeons that remained state of the art until the invention of the telegraph 22 years later.

Aware of Napoleon's defeat nearly a day in advance of anyone else in London, Rothschild made a public show of selling, as if in expectation of bad news. Seeing the alpha wolf of investors in full flight, other investors followed suit, and a selling panic was on. When the price of the bonds had bottomed out, Rothschild stepped back into the market through agents and began buying again. In football terms, Rothschild had run a reverse. While the whole flow of the action was going in one direction, he handed the ball to a wide receiver breaking the other way for daylight. And what daylight it was: a profit of a million pounds, a fortune, and all based on the dynamics of the leader-follower relationship.

Military trainers traditionally have taken this instinct to follow, our built-in desire for direction and orders, and so heightened and refined it that some of their charges would march over a cliff if so directed by their superiors. More aware of the dangers of mob psychology—and chastened by events such as the My Lai massacre during the Vietnam War—modern military trainers set themselves a higher bar: U.S. fighters today are taught to both question bad orders and to follow orders without hesitation.

Soldiers, at least, are following the primal survival instinct. Mohandas Gandhi had to teach his apostles of civil disobedience something far harder: to obey orders at the same time they passively accepted whatever blows fell on them in the fulfillment of their commands. That Gandhi and later Martin Luther King Jr. were able to so effectively use nonviolence in the face of violent responses bears witness both to the power of the herd instinct within humans and to the capacity to harness this power to positive, even noble ends.

As King wrote in his famous *Letter from Birmingham Jail,* "The question is not whether we will be extremist but what kind of extremist will we be. Will we be extremists for hate or will we be extremists for love? Will we be extremists for the preservation of injustice—or will we be extremists for the cause of justice?" It's a matter of what leaders seek to evoke in their followers.

Gandhi and King both sought to stir what Abraham Lincoln described in his first inaugural address as the "better angels of our nature." Absent the firepower to overthrow the British Empire or the manpower to undo centuries of racial animosity, both leaders sought to martial moral power. They asked people to be better than they might individually allow themselves to be, and millions answered the call. John Kennedy struck the same chord in his inaugural address when he told his fellow Americans to "ask not what your country can do for you; ask what you can do for your country," a call to service that gave birth to the Peace Corps and much more.

Demagogues, by contrast, ask their audience to be less than they can be. They know that in the anonymity of the crowd men and women can lose their moral compass—and that in the anonymity of the hood or mask, they can do far worse than that. The demagogue's goal isn't to lift his audience up to a higher level of behavior. It's to bring the crowd down. Demagogues thrive on mobs that have an excess of impetus but little direction. The mass is angry; it's threatened. Someone needs to pay. But angry at whom? Threatened by what? Who is it that should be made to pay? The demagogue's job is to supply the answers: to focus the emotion onto a target until the roar rises for the same form of emotional justice that we looked at in the last section, revenge untempered by reason. To bring the mob to that pitch often requires demonization: of the exploitative rich, of a neighboring country, of some ethnic or racial or religious group within the nation that can be made the scapegoat for all the sins the mob perceives.

Demagogues employ all sorts of symbolism—from banners and flags to youth corps, elaborate titles, and massive rallies. The most effective of them are masters of crowd psychology. But their message is generally the essence of simplicity, announced well in advance of its contemplated solution: You are downtrodden. They are responsible. We need to act.

Look at segments from Chapter 11, "Race & People," of Adolph Hitler's *Mein Kampf*, first published in 1922, and the whole horrible curve of the history of the next quarter century is laid out in stark relief:

> The Jews will therefore remain the unquestioned leaders of the trades union movement so long as a campaign is not undertaken, which must be carried out on gigantic lines, for the enlightenment of the masses; so that they will be enabled better to understand the causes of their misery. Or the same end might be achieved if the government authorities would get rid of the Jew and his work.

Hitler would pound the same drum for 20 and more years. He was relentlessly "on message," as today's spin doctors like to say. All he had to do was convince the mob to believe, and then make the nation itself the mob he directed. For the most part, the Jews he had so succeeded in demonizing weren't able to go anywhere else.

Demagogues move in on mayhem—in Hitler's case, the economic chaos of post–World War I Germany. They play on rumor and suggestion to evoke fear and panic in the mob: a superrace, the myth of Aryan destiny, alleged scurrilous practices of the Jews, the Communists, the Gypsies. Focused on particular enemies, the fear and panic expresses itself as violence and vigilantism. At its worst, unchecked and broadly supported, demagoguery begets wars and genocide.

Like herds of cattle made edgy by the weather or the presence of a natural predator, crowds in a frenzy are unpredictable. Leading them successfully requires a deft touch. Stampedes can break out in any direction. The same demonization that brought the crowd together has a way of coming back to haunt those who do the demonizing.

To marshal public support for the 1991 Persian Gulf War against Iraq, President George Bush and his aides worked hard to paint Iraqi leader Saddam Hussein as a diabolically evil man, a scourge of the region and a threat to global security. (As Henry Kissinger liked to say, it had the added advantage of being true.) The effort worked—and in Saddam,

We humans tend to be herd animals. Where the leader leads, most of us follow along. In this photo, a flock of 2,000 sheep undertake an annual migration over alpine glaciers to their summer pastures in the Austrian North Tyrol.

administration propagandists had an easy and deserving target to work with—but when the war ended with the Mephistopheles of the Middle East still safely entrenched in Baghdad, the very success of the demonization became a measure of the ultimate failure of the Gulf War in many eyes.

Leading a crowd is a little like the job faced by a lion tamer: The chair and the whip need to bring the beast to a convincing frenzy, but when the lion opens its mouth and you stick your head inside, you're hoping against hope that the lion is sufficiently under your control that it won't chomp down.

How do you know if you're in the presence of a demagogue or a genuine leader? The content of the message says a lot: Are you being asked to raise cities or tear them down, open up the wilderness or drive someone else from it? The context of the content matters, too. You needn't understand a word of German to hear the violence and animosity in the speeches of Adolph Hitler. Nor do you need to know English to hear the inner beauty of Abraham Lincoln's Second Inaugural Address. The sound makes sense enough. The "mother test," though, might be the most accurate measure of all: Would you want your mother, or someone else you respect greatly, to know you were standing in a crowd, listening to this leader? Or do you prefer the cloak of anonymity? Are your better angels being awakened, or your worse ones?

~

The tyranny of a multitude is a multiplied tyranny.
—Edmund Burke

Der Führer:
The Voice of the Mob

A leader who tells the crowd what to do always risks having the crowd move in another direction. A leader who makes himself inseparable from the crowd—who seems to be its manifestation, the voice of its collective will—has no such problem. So it was with Adolph Hitler.

From the beginning, Hitler and his henchmen understood that it was the emotional attachments, not the intellectual ones that mattered most to the mob. Make the crowd believe in you in its heart and its head will follow. In 1927, the Nazi Alfred Rosenberg described that year's critical National Socialist Party rally in Nuremberg thus:

> The thousands of S.A. men who marched past their Führer, gazing proudly on him with shining eyes, returned home with the assurance that the Führer was also proud of them. He saw the best German blood go past him. . . . National Socialist thinking is clear and determined. Its values are seen not so much in elegant formulations as in the shining eyes of its brown ranks and in the passion of its adherents.

By 1932, when the Nazi Party gathered in Munich for a rally, the emotional bond between Hitler and his followers had become set in cement: Hitler was the mob. The mob was Hitler. Writer Mary Lee captured the moment memorably for the September 11, 1932, edition of the *New York Times Magazine*.

Thousands of young men with their coats off are lined up in military ranks in the entrance way. The feeling is the same that trembles in the moments just before big doings at a boys' school. A tense excitement, every one silent. Beyond them is the great round arena of the circus building crammed with people, people in every aisle and every doorway, not a cranny that you can crawl through.

Three young men brandish their shirt-sleeves, plunge through the centre of the circle in the middle. "Back!" they cry, "back! The

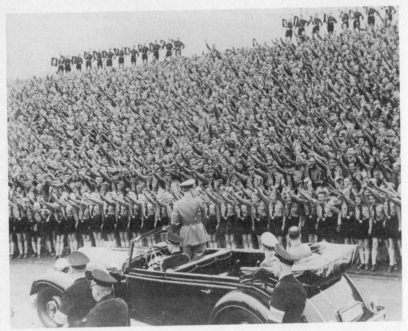

Thousands of youth group members salute der Führer during the Nazi Party's September 1938 Nuremberg Congress. "No European nation has done more for peace than Germany," Hitler told the congress. "No nation has made greater sacrifices." (Hulton Archive/Getty Images)

leader! Here comes he!" You follow them precipitately toward the loggia that you have paid five marks for. Seats? There are no seats; every one filled. People are craning their necks this way, that way. "Der Führer!" they say, "der Führer! Er kommt!" Every one standing, every one stretching to see, every one pushing. "The leader! He comes!" You are squashed back, crushed against the fence of the box you thought you had a seat in. A row of stalwart youths string themselves hand in hand against you, making a passage.

"Heil! Heil!" Ten thousand right hands go up. Tears in the women's eyes, hoarseness in the voices of men. There is an intensity about it, an earnestness. The excitement of a political meeting, but the intensity of people who wait for a wedding or a funeral. "Heil! Heil!" They struggle forward. And then—

A medium-sized, plump man with a small mustache compressed into the very middle of his upper lip is walking past you. A plump, soft, pink and white face, a face with almost no expression in it, a mild face. None of the blustering bombast of Mussolini about this man here. He might be a waiter at a restaurant, a good reliable head porter at a hotel. He edges past quietly, no swagger, no militarism about his gait. A well-nourished burgher he looks, a man who gets not enough exercise but enough fresh air. Why, this man's not a giant!

"Heil! Heil!" He climbs the platform. They shout their heads off. You gaze around at the religiously, almost fanatically, intent crowd. More power in the crowd than in the man here.

He comes forward, an ordinary citizen in a wrinkled blue suit, his face almost expressionless, almost blank; no spark whatever, as yet, in those light eyes. His arms are weak; you feel the right arm aching as he holds it up in salute. He surveys the multitude now like a benign school teacher looking down on her flock. He gestures from the elbow, not the shoulder, or stands with his arms crossed on his stomach, like an old maid, his handkerchief crushed into a small ball in his left hand. What can be the power in this man here?

Martial music. Across the arena, through a narrow lane between the packed spectators, young men come, marching. They are in their shirt sleeves, their right arms extended. They march the goosestep, file directly under the platform on which Hitler stands, and on, through a door, into the darkness beyond. The eyes of each young man are raised to Hitler's. Young eyes, eyes with the idealism of 19. Eyes eager to die for an ideal. Waiting for discipline, waiting to be told what Cause to die for, ready to grasp, to fight for an ideal. The eyes of each man finds the eyes of Hitler, as though he were the embodiment of that ideal.

Hitler's eyes seem to meet the eyes of every young man. He gazes downward, as though he absorbed strength from the passing eyes there. He never smiles. His seriousness reflects the seriousness of the young men, the idealism, the high self-sacrifice of youth—youth that will always march out and be killed, that will follow any one who can appeal to that innate bravery in the race that craves an outlet. That's what he had done, this man: he had caught up this longing of the

THE PIED PIPER OF BERLIN

individual to lose himself for the crowd, this martial instinct, caught it up and led it. The leader, he is, not the instigator.

For a full hour those 3,000 young men march beneath him. Where are they marching, you wonder, as you watch the eager faces. You wonder if they know. Or if he knows.

Slogans are on the wall, in great, blatant letters. "Freedom and bread!" "Death to Marxism so that real socialism may live!" "German labor fights Jewish Marxism so that German socialism can live!"

At last the march is over. The young men are all outside, in the darkness. Hitler comes forward, his hands crossed on his stomach, his handkerchief in his hand. When he gestures, it is by wagging his right hand from the elbow, his forefinger extended, like a woman shaking a finger burned on the stove. Yet, somehow, in the very weakness of his gestures lies his strength. One feels that the man embodies a feeling, reflects a thought, symbolizes an ideal which he is physically not strong enough to convey. One does not feel that Hitler sways the crowd. One feels that the crowd sways Hitler. One feels that he expresses its thoughts, speaks in its words.

~

Demagogues are the mob's lackey.

—Diogenes

Lemming See, Lemming Do

No living thing is more symbolic of blindly following the leader than lemmings. The Norwegian variety particularly is celebrated in legend, cartoons, and photographs for its mass migratory marches, sometimes culminating in what seem to be communal suicidal plunges into the water. But as we see in this short excerpt from Walter Marsden's *The Lemming Years*, it's panic, not a death wish that drives the famous rodents on.

Under exceptional circumstances the lemmings can be seen in a dense mass. They rarely choose when to crowd together. They are probably forced to do so by local topography. A long sea-shore may block off a slow, almost indistinguishable migratory movement and thus dam up the onward flow; or where two arms of a river meet, the lem-

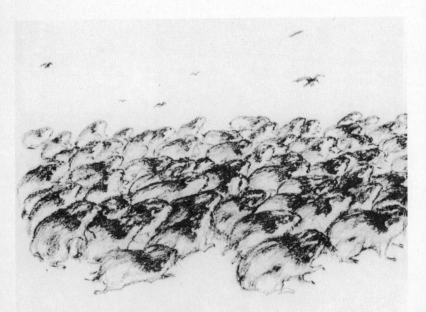

Two to three times each decade, Norwegian lemmings undergo population explosions so extreme that they are driven to pursue food in all directions. When natural boundaries intervene, the lemmings are forced to herd together, sometimes in long columns that have made the small rodents a symbol of obedience to the herd instinct. Occasionally, columns of lemmings will plunge into the ocean and drown, but it's food they're after, not suicide. This illustration by Joan Sandlin is from *The Lemming Condition*, by Alan Arkin.

mings are caught in a sort of hopper when they follow the beach downwards. In such situations the lemmings have to herd together.

These are some of the conditions under which the so-called reckless march can begin. . . . The continuous accumulation of lemmings finally results in overcrowding and the release of panic-like reactions, a type of mass-suggestion. The initiating factors for mass migration include a sort of psychosis, possibly induced by competition and stress.

~

A group of lemmings looks like a pack of individualists compared with Wall Street when it gets a concept in its teeth.

—Warren Buffett

Following the Leader:
The Violence of Nonviolence

Of all the sacrifices a leader can call upon his crowd to make, maybe the greatest is to abandon the instinct to self-defense. That is exactly what Mohandas Gandhi—the Mahatma—did when he launched his campaign of nonviolent civil resistance against India's colonial British masters. In May 1930, Webb Miller was present when some 2,500 of Gandhi's supporters marched on the salt deposits at Dharsana to protest a salt tax levied by the British. Gandhi was in prison at the time. He had been arrested April 6 for manufacturing salt in violation of the British monopoly, but the power of his example was undiminished. Miller sent this report, a classic study of following the leader at any cost, to the *New Freeman*.

The salt deposits were surrounded by ditches filled with water and guarded by 400 native Surat police in khaki shorts and brown turbans. Half-a-dozen British officials commanded them. The police carried *lathis*—five-foot clubs tipped with steel. Inside the stockade twenty-five native riflemen were drawn up.

In complete silence the Gandhi men drew up and halted a hundred yards from the stockade. A picked column advanced from the crowd, waded the ditches, and approached the barbed-wire stockade, which the Surat police surrounded, holding their clubs at the ready. Police officials ordered the marchers to disperse under a recently imposed regulation which prohibited gatherings of more than five persons in any one place. The column silently ignored the warning and slowly walked forward. I stayed with the main body about a hundred yards from the stockade.

Suddenly, at a word of command, scores of native police rushed upon the advancing marchers and rained blows on their heads with their steel-shod *lathis*. Not one of the marchers even raised an arm to fend off the blows. They went down like ten-pins. From where I stood I heard the sickening whacks of the clubs on unprotected skulls. The waiting crowd of watchers groaned and sucked in their breaths in sympathetic pain at every blow.

Those struck down fell sprawling, unconscious or writhing in pain with fractured skulls or broken shoulders. In two or three minutes the ground was quilted with bodies. Great patches of blood widened on their white clothes. The survivors without breaking ranks silently and doggedly marched on until struck down. When every one of the first column had been knocked down stretcher-bearers rushed up unmolested by the police and carried off the injured to a thatched hut which had been arranged as a temporary hospital.

Then another column formed while the leaders pleaded with them to retain their self-control. They marched slowly toward the police. Although every one knew that within a few minutes he would be beaten down, perhaps killed, I could detect no signs of wavering or fear. They marched steadily with heads up, without the encouragement of music or cheering or any possibility that they might escape serious injury or death. The police rushed out and methodically and mechanically beat down the second column. There was no fight, no struggle; the marchers simply walked forward until struck down.

There were no outcries, only groans after they fell. There were not enough stretcher-bearers to carry off the wounded; I saw eighteen injured being carried off simultaneously, while forty-two still lay bleeding on the ground awaiting stretcher-bearers. The blankets used as stretchers were sodden with blood. . . .

∾

I will not choose what many men desire,
Because I will not jump with common spirits,
And rank me with the barbarous multitudes.
　　—William Shakespeare, *The Merchant of Venice*

Leading the Followers:
Fire Within Fire

Gandhi asked his followers to accept violence without resisting so that the British raj might be ended—a form of crowd madness in the pursuit of positive ends. Wagner Dodge asked his followers, 15 U.S. Forest Service Smokejumpers, to do something even more counterintuitive: to step into a circle of fire Dodge had set so that they might be rescued from the raging mountain fire they were fleeing. Gandhi's followers acceded to his request and India won its independence. Dodge's followers didn't accede to his, and nearly all of them died in the pursuing inferno.

What is it that can make a crowd behave in seemingly its own worst interests? Emotion helps. In neither case—Gandhi's or Dodge's—were people being asked to behave in a rational manner. But a track record helps, too. Dodge, the head of the Smokejumpers team, had made the decision that landed his group by parachute behind the fire, a dangerous position. Twice, in confronting the fire, he changed direction until all 15 men were running for their lives. Finally, he really did have the answer: The grass fire he set quickly burned off all the available fuel and left a pocket of oxygen near the ground to survive on while the larger fire roared around, not in the circle. By then, though, his voice had lost all authority.

The date is August 5, 1949. The scene: the Mann Gulch Fire in the Montana wilderness. Dodge's team has been on the ground for two hours. Within minutes, all of the men save Dodge and two sprinters—Walter Rumsey and Robert Sallee, who managed to outrun the fire—will be dead or fatally injured. This excerpt is from Norman Maclean's account of that day, *Young Men and Fire*.

Dodge had come out of the timber ahead of his crew, with the fire just behind. He saw that in front was high dry grass that would burn very fast, saw for the first time the top of the ridge at what he judged to be about two hundred yards above, put two and two together and decided that he and his crew couldn't make the two hundred yards, and almost instantly invented what was to become known as the "escape fire" by lighting a patch of bunch grass with a gofer match.

In so doing, he started an argument that would remain hot long after the fire.

At the time it probably made no sense to anyone but Dodge to light a fire right in front of the main fire. It couldn't act as a backfire; there wasn't any time to run a fire-line along its upgulch edge to prevent it from being just an advance arm of the main fire. Uncontrolled, instead of being a backfire it might act as a spot fire on its way upgulch and bring fire from behind that much closer and sooner to the crew.

Dodge was starting to light a second fire with a second match when he looked up and saw that his first fire had already burned one hundred square feet of grass up the slope. "This way," he kept calling to his crew behind. "This way." Many of the crew, as they came in sight of him, must have asked themselves, What's this dumb bastard doing? The smoke lifted twice so that everyone had a good chance to ask the question.

The crew must have been stretched nearly all the way from the edge of the timber to the center of the grassy clearing ahead, where Dodge was lighting his fire. Rumsey and Sallee say that the men did not panic, but by now all began to fear death and were in a race with it. The line had already assumed that erratic spread customary in a race where everything is at stake. When it comes to racing with death, all men are not created equal.

At the edge of the timber the crew for the first time could have seen to the head of the gulch where the fire, having moved up the south side of the gulch, was now circling. From the open clearing they also could see partway toward the bottom of the gulch, where it was presumably rocks that were exploding in smoke. They didn't have to look behind—they could feel the heat going to their lungs straight through their backs. From the edge of the clearing they could also see the top of the ridge for the first time. It wasn't one and a half miles away; to them it seemed only two hundred yards or so away. Why was this son of a bitch stopping to light another fire? . . .

The smoke will never roll away and leave a clear picture of the head of the line reaching Dodge and his burned bunch grass. Dodge later pictured the crew as strung out about 150 feet with at least eight men close enough together and close enough to him so that he could try to explain to them—but without stopping them—that they could not survive unless they got into his grass fire. At the Review, he made very clear that he believed there was not enough time left for them to make it to the top of the hill, and events came close to supporting his belief. In the roar and smoke he kept "hollering" at them—he was sure that at least those closest to him heard him and that those behind understood him from his actions. In smoke that swirled and made sounds, there was a pause, then somebody said, "To hell with that, I'm getting out of here," and a line of them followed the voice.

The line all headed in the same direction, but in the smoke Dodge could not see whether any of them looked back at him. He estimated that the main fire would hit them in thirty seconds.

~

With a mob, everything depends on the first impression made upon it.

—Napoleon

In Honoré Daumier's drawing *Camile Desmoulins au Palais Royale,* a young author calls French citizens to arms against the crown on July 12, 1789, in front of the Royal Palace. Desmoulins would eventually be sentenced to death by the revolutionary tribunal. He was executed April 5, 1794.

Off with Their Heads

Think of the American Revolution, and one is likely to conjure up an image of Washington accepting Cornwallis's surrender at Yorktown or of Jefferson, John Adams, and the others gathered in Philadelphia's Liberty Hall to finalize the wording on that great document, the Declaration of Independence. Think of the French Revolution, which followed a decade later, and a very different set of images is likely to come to mind: the guillotine, baskets of severed human heads, the blood lust of the masses.

The difference is in part the result of the myths that have grown up around both events. Tory sympathizers were drawn and quartered in the town squares of America just as high purpose rose above the angry clamor of Parisian streets. But the difference also goes to leadership, and its absence. America had its Founding Fathers. France had its mob, and without leadership, the mob knew nothing more than to repay the violence of the past with the horror of the present.

"Along the Paris streets, the death-carts tumble, hollow and harsh," Charles Dickens wrote in *A Tale of Two Cities*. "Six tumbrils carry the day's wine to La Guillotine. All the devouring and insatiate monsters imagined since imagination could record itself are fused in the one realisation, Guillotine." The following account of the storming of the Bastille—July 14, 1789—comes from Charles Morris's *Historical Tales*, first published in 1893.

"To the Bastille! To the Bastille!" was the cry. Paris surged with an ungovernable mob. Month by month, week by week, day by day, since the meeting of the States-General—called into being to provide money for the king, and kept in being to provide government for the people—the revolutionary feeling had grown, alike among the delegates and among the citizens. Now the population of Paris was aroused, the unruly element of the city was in the streets, their wrath directed against the prison-fortress, the bulwark of feudalism, the stronghold of oppression, the infamous keeper of the dark secrets of the kings of France. The people had always feared, always hated it, and now against its sullen walls was directed the torrent of their wrath.

The Bastille was the visible emblem of that oppression. It was an armed fortress threatening Paris. The cannon on its walls frowned defiance to the people. Momentarily the wrath of the multitude grew stronger. The electors of the Third Estate sent a message to Delaunay, governor of the Bastille, asking him to withdraw the cannons, the sight of which infuriated the people, and promising, if he would do this, to restrain the mob.

The advice was wise; the governor was not. The messengers were long absent; the electors grew uneasy; the tumult in the streets increased. At length the deputation returned, bringing word that the governor pledged himself not to fire on the people, unless forced to do so in self-defence. Even while the electors were reporting the governor's evasive message to the crowd around the Hotel de Ville the cannon of the Bastille were roaring defiance to the people of Paris!

That shot was fatal to Delaunay. The citizens heard it with rage. "Treason!" was the cry. "To the Bastille! To the Bastille!" again rose the shout. Surging onward in an irresistible mass, the furious crowd poured through the streets, and soon surrounded the towering walls of the detested prison-fortress. A few bold men had already cut the chains of the first drawbridge, and let it fall. Across it rushed the multitude to attack the second bridge.

The fortress was feebly garrisoned, having but thirty Swiss soldiers and eighty invalids for its defence.

A chance shot was fired from the crowd; the soldiers answered with a volley; several men were wounded; other shots came from the people; the governor gave orders to fire the cannon; the struggle had begun.

It proved a short one. Companies of the National Guard were brought up to restrain the mob—the soldiers broke from their ranks and joined it. Two of their sub-officers, Elie and Hullin by name, put themselves at the head of the furious crowd and led the people to the assault on the fortress.

Delaunay proposed to capitulate, saying that he would yield if he and his men were allowed to march out with arms and honor. The proposition was received with shouts of sarcastic laughter.

"Life and safety are all we can promise you," answered Elie. "This I engage on the word of an officer."

Delaunay at this ordered the second drawbridge to be lowered and the gates to be opened. In poured the mass, precipitating themselves in fury upon that hated fortress, rushing madly through all its halls and passages, breaking its cell-doors with hammer blows, releasing captives some of whom had been held there in hopeless misery for half a lifetime, unearthing secrets which added to their revengeful rage.

Elie and Hullin had promised the governor his life. They miscalculated their power over their savage followers. Before they had gone far they were fighting hand to hand with the multitude for the safety of their prisoner. At the Place de Greve, Hullin seized the governor in his strong arms and covered his bare head with a hat, with the hope of concealing his features from the people. In a moment more he was hurled down and trodden under foot, and on struggling to his feet saw the head of Delaunay carried on a pike.

Two months after the March 1917 abdication of Tsar Nicholas II, Russians gather in Moscow to celebrate May Day—a moment of relative calm in what was to prove a degenerating cycle of violence. Six months later, Bolsheviks seized control of the government in a violent coup, and in July 1918, Nicholas and other members of the royal family were murdered in the house in the Urals where they were being held.

A Little Knowledge Is a Dangerous Thing

Some people know so much that they can't be led where their hearts don't want to go. Others know just enough to fall for whatever the crowd seems to be buying into. The key consideration—and every citizen's obligation—is to do due diligence. Whether it's stocks or politics or the alleged guilt of an entire class of people that's at stake, we all need to ask ourselves carefully and unflinchingly: What am I really being pulled into? In this brief parable from his book *Fables for Our Time,* James Thurber introduces us to a perfect dupe: "The Fairly Intelligent Fly."

A large spider in an old house built a beautiful web in which to catch flies. Every time a fly landed on the web and was entangled in it the spider devoured him, so that when another fly came along he would think the web was a safe and quiet place in which to rest. One day a fairly intelligent fly buzzed around above the web so long without lighting that the spider appeared and said, "Come on down." But the fly was too clever for him and said, "I never light where I don't see other flies and I don't see any other flies in your house." So he flew away until he came to a place where there were a great many flies. He was about to settle down among them when a bee buzzed up and said, "Hold it, stupid, that's flypaper. All those flies are trapped." "Don't be silly," said the fly, "they're dancing." So he settled down and became stuck to the flypaper with all the other flies.

Moral: There is no safety in numbers, or in anything else.

～

No man who depends upon the caprice of the ignorant rabble can be accounted great.

—Cicero

Hans Christian Andersen's Tale
of Leaders & Yes-Men

In his brief poem "Epitaph on a Tyrant," W.H. Auden caught with rueful humor what happens when the power of a leader is absolute:

Perfection, of a kind, was what he was after,
And the poetry he invented was easy to understand;
He knew human folly like the back of his hand,
And was greatly interested in armies and fleets;
When he laughed, respectable senators burst with laughter,
And when he cried the little children died in the streets.

Hans Christian Andersen's famous story "The Emperor's New Clothes" is a gentler approach to the same end. When rule is absolute, when the only answer is "yes," when the people are nothing more than an expression of their leader's whims and fancies, folly can follow as easily as horror.

Once upon a time an Emperor was so fond of fine new clothes that he spent all his money upon them, that he might be very grand. He did not care about his soldiers or the theatre, and only liked to drive out and show off his new clothes. He had a coat for every hour of the day; and just as they say of a king, "He is in council," so it was always said of him, "The Emperor is in the wardrobe."

In the great city in which he lived many strangers came every day. One day two rogues came. They said they were weavers and declared they could weave the finest stuff anyone could imagine. Not only were their colors and patterns uncommonly beautiful, they said, but the clothes made of the stuff possessed the wonderful quality that they became invisible to anyone who was unfit for the office he held or was very stupid.

"Those would be most unusual clothes!" thought the Emperor. "If I wore those, I should be able to find out what men in my empire are not fit for the places they have; I could tell the clever ones from the dunces. Yes, the stuff must be woven for me directly!"

And he gave the two rogues a great deal of cash, so that they might begin their work at once.

As for them, they put up two looms, and pretended to be working; but they had nothing at all on their looms. They at once demanded the finest silk and the costliest gold; this they put into their own pockets, and worked at the empty looms till late into the night.

A few weeks passed. Then the Emperor said to himself, "I should like to know how far they have got on with the stuff." But he felt quite uncomfortable when he thought that those who were not fit for their offices could not see it. He believed, of course, that he had nothing to fear for himself, but he preferred first to send someone else to see how matters stood.

"I will send my honest old Minister to the weavers," thought the Emperor. "He can judge best how the stuff looks, for he has sense, and no one understands his office better than he."

So the good old Minister went out into the hall where the two rogues sat working at the empty looms.

"Mercy on us!" thought the old Minister, and he opened his eyes wide. I cannot see anything at all! Can I indeed be so stupid? I never thought that, and not a soul must know it. Am I not fit for my office? No, it will never do for me to tell that I could not see the stuff."

"Haven't you anything to say about it?" asked one of the rogues, as he went on weaving. "Oh, it is charming—quite enchanting!" answered the old Minister, as he peered through his spectacles. "What a fine pattern, and what colors! Yes, I shall tell the Emperor that I am very much pleased with it."

Now the rogues asked for more money, and silk and gold, which they declared they wanted for weaving. They put it all into their own pockets, and not a thread was put upon the loom; they continued to work at the empty frames as before.

The Emperor soon sent another honest officer of the court to see how the weaving was going on and if the stuff would soon be ready. He fared just like the first: he looked and looked, but, as there was nothing to be seen but the empty looms, he could see nothing.

"Isn't that a pretty piece of stuff?" asked the two rogues; and they displayed and explained the handsome pattern which was not there at all.

"I am not stupid!" thought the man. "Yet it must be that I am not fit for my office. If that is the case, I must not let it be noticed." And so he praised the stuff which he did not see, and expressed his pleasure at the beautiful colors and charming pattern. "Yes, it is enchanting," he told the Emperor.

All the people in the town were talking of the gorgeous stuff. The Emperor wished to see it himself while it was still upon the loom. With a whole crowd of chosen men, among whom were also the two honest statesmen who had already been there, he went to the two cunning rogues, who were now weaving with might and main without fibre or thread.

"Isn't that splendid?" said the two statesmen, who had already been there once. "Doesn't your Majesty approve of the pattern and the colors?" And they pointed to the empty loom, for they thought that the others could see the stuff.

"What's this?" thought the Emperor. "I can see nothing at all? That is terrible. Am I stupid? Am I not fit to be Emperor? That would be the most dreadful thing that could happen to me. Oh, it is very pretty!" he said aloud. "It has our highest approval." And he nodded in a contented way, and gazed at the empty loom, for he would not say that he saw nothing. Those whom he had with him looked and looked, and saw nothing, any more than the rest; but, like the Emperor, they said, "That is pretty!" and advised him to wear the splendid new clothes for the first time at the great procession that was to take place the following week. "It is splendid, excellent!" went from mouth to mouth. On all sides there seemed to be general rejoicing, and the Emperor gave the rogues the title of Imperial Court Weavers.

The whole night before the morning on which the procession was to take place, the rogues were up, keeping more than sixteen candles burning. The people could see that they were hard at work, completing the Emperor's new clothes. They pretended to take the stuff down from the loom: they made great slashes in the air with their scissors; they sewed with needles without thread; and at last they said, "Now the clothes are ready!"

The Emperor came himself with his noblest cavaliers; and the two rogues lifted their arms as if they were holding something, and said,

"All those in favor say 'Aye.'"
"Aye."   *"Aye."*   *"Aye."*   *"Aye."*
         "Aye."   *"Aye."*

"See, here are the trousers! Here is the coat! Here is the cloak!" and so on. "It is as light as a spider's web: one would think one had nothing on; but that is just the beauty of it."

"Yes," said all the cavaliers; but they could not see anything, for nothing was there.

"Will your Imperial Majesty please take off your clothes?" said the rogues. "Then we will put on you the new clothes here in front of the great mirror."

The Emperor took off his clothes, and the rogues pretended to put on him each new garment as it was ready; and the Emperor turned round and round before the mirror.

"Oh, how fine they look! How well they fit!" said everybody. "What a pattern! What colors! That is a splendid outfit."

"They are standing outside with the canopy which is to be borne above your Majesty in the procession!" announced the Master of the Ceremonies.

"Well, I am ready," replied the Emperor. "Does it not suit me well?" And then he turned again to the mirror, for he wanted it to appear as if he contemplated his adornment with great interest.

The two chamberlains who were to carry the train stooped down with their hands toward the floor, just as if they were picking up the mantle; they then pretended to be holding something in the air.

So the Emperor went in procession under the rich canopy, and everyone in the streets said, "How elegant are the Emperor's new clothes! What a train he has to his mantle! How it fits him!" No one would let it be known that he could see nothing, for that would have shown that he was not fit for his office, or was very stupid.

"But he has nothing on!" a little child cried out at last.

"Just hear what the innocent says!" said the father. And each person began whispering to another what the child had said.

"But he has nothing on!" said all the people at last. That touched the Emperor, for it seemed to him that they were right; but he thought to himself, "I must go through with the procession." And so he held himself a little higher, and the chamberlains held on tighter than ever, and carried the train which did not exist at all.

~

Away, and mock the time with fairest show:
False face must hide what the false heart doth know.
—Shakespeare, Macbeth

The Mind of the Mob: Stupidity Accumulates, but Also Heroism

Every exploration of the psychology of crowds owes a heavy debt to the French philosopher and politician Gustave Le Bon and his pioneering 1897 book *The Crowd: A Study of the Popular Mind.* This book is no exception. Le Bon wrote in the often grandiose style of his age, but his observations on crowds, on mob behavior, on leaders and followers are often timeless. Herewith, a sampler from Book I, "The Mind of Crowds."

- Under certain given circumstances, and only under those circumstances, an agglomeration of men presents new characteristics very different from those of the individuals composing it. The sentiments and ideas of all the persons in the gathering take one and the same direction, and their conscious personality vanishes. A collective mind is formed, doubtless transitory, but presenting very clearly defined characteristics. The gathering has thus become what, in the absence of a better expression, I will call an organised crowd, or, if the term is considered preferable, a psychological crowd. It forms a single being, and is subjected to the *law of the mental unity of crowds.*

- The most striking peculiarity presented by a psychological crowd is the following: Whoever be the individuals that compose it, however like or unlike be their mode of life, their occupations, their character, or their intelligence, the fact that they have been transformed into a crowd puts them in possession of a sort of collective mind which makes them feel, think, and act in a manner quite different from that in which each individual of them would feel, think, and act were he in a state of isolation. There are certain ideas and feelings which do not come into being, or do not transform themselves into acts except in the case of individuals forming a crowd. The psychological crowd is a provisional being formed of heterogeneous elements, which for a moment are combined, exactly as the cells which constitute a living body form by their reunion a new being which displays characteristics very different from those possessed by each of the cells singly.

- In the collective mind the intellectual aptitudes of the individuals, and in consequence their individuality, are weakened. The heterogeneous is swamped by the homogeneous, and the unconscious qualities obtain the upper hand.

- In crowds it is stupidity and not mother-wit that is accumulated.

- We know today that by various processes an individual may be brought into such a condition that, having entirely lost his conscious personality, he obeys all the suggestions of the operator who has deprived him of it, and commits acts in utter contradiction with his character and habits. The most careful observations seem to prove that an individual emerged for some length of time in a crowd in action soon finds himself—either in consequence of the magnetic influence given out by the crowd, or from some other cause of which we are ignorant—in a special state, which much resembles the state of fascination in which the hypnotized individual finds himself. . . . The conscious personality has entirely vanished; will and discernment are lost.

- By the mere fact that he forms part of an organized crowd, a man descends several rungs in the ladder of civilization. Isolated, he may be a cultivated individual; in a crowd, he is a barbarian—that is, a creature acting by instinct. He possesses the spontaneity, the violence, the ferocity, and also the enthusiasm and heroism of primitive beings, whom he further tends to resemble by the facility with which he allows himself to be impressed by words and images—which would be entirely without action on each of the isolated individuals composing the crowd—and to be induced to commit acts contrary to his most obvious interests and his best-known habits. An individual in a crowd is a grain of sand amid other grains of sand, which the wind stirs up at will.

- It is not only by his acts that the individual in a crowd differs essentially from himself. Even before he has entirely lost his

independence, his ideas and feelings have undergone a transformation, and the transformation is so profound as to change
the miser into a spendthrift, the skeptic into a believer, the honest man into a criminal, and the coward into a hero.

- The conclusion to be drawn from what precedes is that the
  crowd is always intellectually inferior to the isolated individual but that, from the point of view of feelings and of the acts
  these feelings provoke, the crowd may, according to circumstances, be better or worse than the individual. All depends on
  the nature of the suggestion to which the crowd is exposed.
- Doubtless a crowd is often criminal, but also it is often heroic.
  It is crowds rather than isolated individuals that may be
  induced to run the risk of death to secure the triumph of a
  creed or an idea, that may be fired with enthusiasm for glory
  and honor, that are led on—almost without bread and without
  arms, as in the age of the Crusades—to deliver the tomb of
  Christ from the infidel or ... to defend the fatherland. Such
  heroism is without doubt somewhat unconscious, but it is of
  such heroism that history is made.

~

The mob has nothing to lose, everything to gain.
—Goethe

A crowd can be as powerful a force for good as it is for evil. In this photo, taken in Prague on August 21, 1968, Czech citizens gathered outside the state radio station confront the first Warsaw Pact tank to roll into the city.

Two more examples of a crowd using its collective strength to achieve positive ends. Above, civil-rights leaders and supporters on the famous march from Selma, Alabama, to the state capital at Montgomery in late March 1965, shortly after a bloody confrontation in Selma left one protester dead. Below, the Women's Srike for Equality takes to the streets of New York City on August 26, 1970.

Rudyard Kipling on Leading and Following

Here is some of the best advice I've ever run across in four and more decades of contemplating the madness of crowds: Rudyard Kipling's poem "If." It should be engraved in every trading room, office, and governmental chamber in the land. And it should be carried in our hearts and minds as well.

If you can keep your head when all about you
Are losing theirs and blaming it on you;
If you can trust yourself when all men doubt you,
But make allowance for their doubting too;
If you can wait and not be tired by waiting,
Or, being lied about, don't deal in lies,
Or, being hated, don't give way to hating,
And yet don't look too good, nor talk too wise;

If you can dream—and not make dreams your master;
If you can think—and not make thoughts your aim;
If you can meet with triumph and disaster
And treat those two imposters just the same;
If you can bear to hear the truth you've spoken
Twisted by knaves to make a trap for fools,
Or watch the things you gave your life to broken,
And stoop and build 'em up with wornout tools;

If you can make one heap of all your winnings
And risk it on one turn of pitch-and-toss,
And lose, and start again at your beginnings
And never breathe a word about your loss;
If you can force your heart and nerve and sinew
To serve your turn long after they are gone,
And so hold on when there is nothing in you
Except the Will which says to them: "Hold on";

If you can talk with crowds and keep your virtue,
Or walk with kings—nor lose the common touch;
If neither foes nor loving friends can hurt you;
If all men count with you, but none too much;

If you can fill the unforgiving minute
With sixty seconds' worth of distance run—
Yours is the Earth and everything that's in it,
And—which is more—you'll be a Man, my son!

Keeping Your Head When All About You Are Losing Theirs

In a democracy such as ours, every man is a king, but not all kings are created equal. Any organization—whether it's a basketball team, a steel company, or a school—has to be pyramidical to prosper and survive. Life has leaders and life has followers, and there will always be more of the latter than the former. The question isn't whether everyone is going to have an equal voice in every enterprise. The real question is how best to exercise your obligations in those situations in which you find yourself called to lead and in those in which you're asked to follow or required to walk behind. The following are some rules to keep in mind for each role.

For followers:

- Question authority. Just because a dictate comes from on high doesn't mean it comes from the high road or is imbued with the highest motives.

- Don't be afraid to speak up. If leadership is willing to listen, you might just make the difference. If it's not willing, you could be marching in the wrong parade.

- Keep a close eye on momentum. The more you feel yourself being propelled forward against your will by those around you, the more you need to dig your heels in and puzzle things out for yourself. Would you make this investment or take part in this demonstration on your own? Or are you drawing your courage and conviction from the crowd?

- Put yourself in charge, at least in your own mind. What are you leading people toward or away from? And why? The more you can see your actions simultaneously from inside and outside, the greater your depth perception will be.

- Trust instinct. Reason has a way of deserting us when the crowd gets moving, but instinct seldom does. A course of action should not only make sense. It should feel right, deep down.

For leaders:

- Tolerate insubordination—not totally, but enough so that good ideas and course corrections can bubble up from below. A leader surrounded by yes-men hears only one word.

- Practice humility, too, and don't forget basic physical principles. When you're sitting on top of the pyramid, you're being held up by everyone below.
- One question: Is the course of action you're pursuing for your own glory or for the good of those who are following you? Leaders get more rewards, but they have to be willing to accept the responsibility the crowd has placed in them and exercise it to the common benefit.
- A second question: Have you laid the groundwork so that those below you will follow you when the going gets tough and there's no time for debate? Trust isn't imposed. It's the accumulation of hundreds of small acts.
- And a third one: Are you really in charge, or just parroting someone else's phrases and following a well-worn trail? Leading is about more than sitting on the head horse or occupying the biggest suite of offices. Leadership requires vision and the courage to go the course alone if need be.

In the final analysis, whether we're leaders or followers, the madness of crowds is a question of individual character: how much we yield to the collective impulse and how much we retain for ourselves, how much we make up our own mind and how much we allow others to make our choices for us. Don't fight the crowd just to be on the outside—crowds have good impulses as well as bad ones—but don't go along just to get along either.

Keep your own counsel, have faith in your own capacities, make the important decisions in solitude not in the tumult of the moment, and you can't go too far wrong, whether you're risking your money, your vote, or your honor.

$\sim$

Let us not follow where the path may lead.
Let us go instead where there is no path.
                                        —Japanese proverb

Acknowledgments

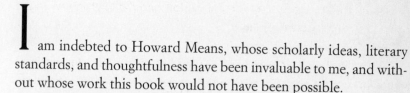

I am indebted to Howard Means, whose scholarly ideas, literary standards, and thoughtfulness have been invaluable to me, and without whose work this book would not have been possible.

For their help in dozens of ways, I thank Jeffrey Hoone and Germaine Clair. Their early effort and ideas helped form this book. Special thanks are due Peter Bernstein and Peter Dougherty for their generous sharing of time and encouragement.

For his advice and a lifetime of friendship, I especially thank William Safire. I am also indebted to my son, David, for his perspective and early comments, and to my daughter, Lauren.

Many thanks to my longtime friend and literary agent, Morton L. Janklow, and his associate, Anne Sibbald, for their oversight, and to my editor at John Wiley, Airie Stuart, and her associate Emily Conway for their guidance and professional insight.

I am extremely grateful for the work of Virginia Creeden, who cleared rights and permissions, and to Claire Huismann and Impressions Book and Journal Services, who helped give the book final shape. Marianne Sammarco, my administrative assistant for more than twelve years, was steadfast in her commitment and patience as was her assistant, Jacquie Carroll.

Foremost and always, thanks to my wife, Joyce.

Text Credits

Illustration and Photo Credits

Part 1

1: *Harper's Weekly,* February 1890. Run on a Bank. The New York Public Library. **9:** © The *New Yorker* Collection 1998 Leo Cullum from cartoonbank.com. All rights reserved. **11:** Pieter Holsteyn the Younger. **14:** © The *New Yorker* Collection 2001 Peter Steiner from cartoonbank.com. All rights reserved. **17:** *Frank Leslie's Illustrated Newspaper,* New York, April 12, 1879, Leadville Colorado Town Center. The New York Public Library. **24:** *Harper's Weekly,* February 1890. Run on a Bank. The New York Public Library. **26:** © Henri Cartier-Bresson/Magnum Photos. **32:** © Bettmann/CORBIS. **36:** © The *New Yorker* Collection 1999 David Sipress from cartoonbank.com. All rights reserved. **39:** Doonesbury © 1998 by G.B. Trudeau. Reprinted with permission of Universal Press Syndicate. All rights reserved. **44:** © Seymour Chwast, the Pushpin Group. **48:** Michael Klein.

Part 2

53: AP/Wide World Photo. **60:** The Granger Collection, New York. **63:** © Punch, Ltd. **64:** George Bellows, *The Crowd,* 1923. **73:** AP/Wide World Photo. **74:** © Bettmann/CORBIS. **75:** © Hulton-Deutsch Collections/CORBIS. **77:** © The *New Yorker* Collection 1985 Charles Addams from cartoonbank.com. All rights reserved. **79:** E. Hausner/*The New York Times.* **83:** © The *New Yorker* Collection 1992 Tom Cheney from cartoonbank.com. All rights reserved. **86:** Hulton Archive/Getty Images. **92:** © The *New Yorker* Collection 1990 Edward Koren from cartoonbank.com. All rights reserved.

Part 3

97: George Grosz, Pandemonium, 1914. Courtesy Moeller Achim Fine Art Ltd. **101:** *Harper's Weekly,* New York, May 31, 1883. The New York Public Library. **106:** ©

Part 4

Part 5